KT-420-547

GYM CLIMBING:
Maximizing Your
Indoor Experience

Contents

Acknowledgments

There are countless people who made this project possible. Without Earth Treks' Climbing Centers, I never would have had the opportunity to work with such a great staff and eager students who have helped mold my experiences as an instructor and climber. Thank you to all the students who have given me the opportunity to help them better their understanding of climbing, as well as mine.

Many thanks to Bill Pelkey, Brad Dorough, Doug Madara, Leigh Saunders, Russ Clune, and LaSportiva for their friendship and support throughout my climbing endeavors. Thank you also to Adrian Ballinger, Brad Mering, Charlotte Jouette, Chris Nance, Chris Warner, Dave Hudson, Eric J. Horst, Mary Metz, Mike Wolfert, S. Peter Lewis, Sam Hanks, Sue Borchardt, and particularly my editor, Julie Van Pelt, for your contributions to this book. To my dad, I finally see the value in rewriting all those sentences when I was a kid.

Most importantly, I express my deepest gratitude to my wife, Elizabeth, who was there for every step of this journey, and I look forward to a lifetime of more adventure together.

Introduction

Founded in Seattle in 1987, the Vertical Club climbing gym was the first to move the traditionally outdoor sport of rock climbing into an indoor arena. Now, less than twenty years later, millions of people around the world have discovered the physical and mental challenges, as well as the great social setting, of indoor climbing. To meet and fuel this demand, hundreds of commercial climbing gyms have sprung up throughout the United States and Europe, together forming a multimillion-dollar industry. Nearly every state in the United States has at least one indoor climbing facility, with many cities boasting several gyms apiece. In addition, countless universities, colleges, and fitness centers have also constructed artificial climbing walls for recreation and fitness.

Despite the wildfire-like spread of indoor climbing, anyone who has tried or seen climbing knows that it is not a pastime to be taken on lightly. Climbing safely requires practice and knowledge, which in turn requires solid, clear instruction in all of the necessary skills. Although many indoor climbing facilities offer basic and even advanced-skills classes, these are often insufficient to support the growth and development of a novice into an experienced, comfortable, competent climber. And unlike most other sports, climbers generally do not join teams through which they can receive coaching. Learning the ins and outs of climbing beyond the basics is usually an exercise in both apprenticeship and self-instruction.

To support this unique and exciting learning process, the Mountaineers Outdoor Expert Series presents *Gym Climbing: Maximizing Your Indoor Experience*, a manual for novices just entering the world of indoor climbing as well as for more experienced climbers who want to improve their technique, strength, endurance, or knowledge of safety systems. *Gym Climbing* responds to a demand by indoor climbers for a complete reference, one that reflects the fact that gym climbing has evolved from a foul-weather alternative to outdoor climbing into a sport in itself, complete with its own unique language, techniques, and skills. With the publication of this book, indoor climbers will no longer have to rely on the occasional chapter in books covering the full extent of the sport of rock climbing. Rather, this reference will support both novice and experienced climbers in mastering the art of indoor climbing.

Novice enthusiasts will value *Gym Climbing* for its broad and deep treatment of all aspects of indoor rock climbing, including everything from information needed to make decisions about gear investments to details on proper top-rope systems management and movement technique. More advanced indoor climbers will appreciate chapters on topics such as indoor leading and performance. A beginner will not need another reference for indoor climbing skills and techniques because this book grows with the climber. As the user of *Gym Climbing* masters skills and techniques, he or she will be ready to apply the more advanced skills covered, like indoor lead climbing and belaying.

Realizing the training benefits as well as the social aspects of indoor climbing, more-experienced outdoor rock climbers are now climbing in gyms. As this advanced crowd will tell you, there is no better way to develop climbing strength, technique, and endurance than actually climbing, and indoor climbing allows for maximum training in minimal time. *Gym Climbing* presents the most comprehensive set of technique and training exercises of any climbing reference published to date. All exercises described have been used by hundreds of climbers coached by the author, who has then taken the experiences of those climbers to improve upon and adapt the exercises as needed. Outdoor traditionalists will also find this book helpful because, even for veteran rock climbers, the indoor climbing approach to belay skills, movement technique, and training can leave an outdoor climber lost in an indoor world. This book will help the "reverse" transition of climbing on real rock to pulling on plastic.

Finally, it should be noted that although this book is designed as a complete reference for the indoor climber, mastering the skills presented is not a substitute for sound judgment, experience, and personal instruction. Ultimately, every climber is responsible for his or her safety in this activity where participants take risks that are inherent to the sport of climbing. It should also be noted that *Gym Climbing* does not prepare a climber to take on the challenges of climbing outside on real rock. The reference for transitioning from indoor climbing to outdoor climbing is the Mountaineers' *Climbing: From Gym to Crag* by S. Peter Lewis and Dan Cauthorn.

HOW TO USE THIS BOOK

The contents of *Gym Climbing* are organized to reflect the climbing learning process, beginning with an overview of indoor climbing facilities and then moving on to discuss equipment, the basics of toproping (climbing on ropes attached to preset anchors), climbing technique, lead climbing (setting the anchor as you climb up), bouldering (climbing low to the ground unroped), and training for improved performance. Reading this book from cover to cover may instantly gratify the enthusiastic learner, but more gradually working through and mastering the skills described in each chapter will be the most effective way to ensure safe and steady improvement. As climbing skills and ability develop, reviewing past sections before moving on is recommended to prevent the formation of bad habits, which we all know are very hard to break.

KEY EXERCISES

Throughout the book there will be Key Exercises. For all readers, these exercises will provide an opportunity to practice and master skills before progressing or revisiting those skills that still require improvement. There is a saying that the worst place to learn how to play golf is during an actual game of golf. In other words, the activity is too complicated and complex to learn the fundamental skills in a live situation and therefore should first be practiced in a controlled environment that permits focus on individual skills. The same is true for indoor climbing, except that the consequences of inexperience can be considerably more dangerous.

Gym Climbing presents Key Exercises that promote development of specific skills required for safe climbing and belaying in an indoor climbing environment. Covering everything from top-rope belaying to bouldering techniques, these exercises are designed to break the greater picture of climbing into smaller, more manageable pieces. Practicing these exercises also allows the reader to identify personal strengths and weaknesses and to build confidence before applying these skills in a "live" climbing situation.

All of the Key Exercises were performed at Earth Treks' Climbing Center in Timonium, Maryland. An indoor climbing facility whose focus is instruction, Earth Treks designed a climbing area specifically for teaching, complete with skill practice areas equipped with anchors, carabiners, bolts, or holds needed for specific exercises. Even if your climbing gym does not have gear or holds established to practice the Key Exercises, performing them should still be quick and easy with a little imagination. Climbing gyms want safe climbers and progressing clients, so helping you set up Key Exercise areas is in their best interest. Other than some technique skills, all Key Exercises are designed to be performed near the ground.

A NOTE ABOUT SAFETY

Safety is an important concern in all climbing activities. No book can alert you to every hazard or anticipate the limitations of every reader. The descriptions of techniques and procedures in this book are intended to provide general information. This is not a complete text on indoor climbing technique. Nothing substitutes for formal instruction, routine practice, and plenty of experience. When you follow any of the procedures described here, you assume responsibility for your own safety. Use this book as a general guide to further information.

—*The Mountaineers Books*

CHAPTER 1

Indoor Climbing

Climbing is a unique activity that people of different abilities and ages can enjoy together. It takes us out of our normal horizontal world and into a vertical environment that is physically demanding and mentally challenging. Some climbers choose to reach high peaks of the world, like the summit of Mount Everest. Others enjoy climbing at the local rock faces after work with their friends. And still others choose to climb up frozen waterfalls. The avenues of climbing are extremely varied, each with its own unique environment, set of technical skills, and physical demands.

Gym climbing, climbing indoors on fabricated climbing-wall structures, is the fastest growing aspect of climbing. There are several hundred indoor climbing gyms in the United States and Europe and that number is constantly on the rise. Ask gym climbers why they choose to climb indoors and a typical response is "because it's fun."

The attraction stems from the physical, mental, and even social benefits that gym climbing provides.

Indoor climbing challenges both the body and the mind. Although climbing may be perceived as an upper body–intensive activity that develops Herculean shoulders and Popeye forearms, every major muscle group in the body contributes to climbing's physical demands. Tough climbs done even with good technique can leave your whole body sore the next day. The full-body aspect of climbing not only develops muscle stabilization and increases strength, but also can improve your joint flexibility and range of motion. And the physical aspect of climbing is just a tip of the iceberg.

Climbing is as much a cerebral activity as it is physical. The excitement comes from the problem-solving skills needed to figure out a particular movement and then actually complete that move. You have to anticipate what hold you want to grab next or how to shift your weight over your feet. The 20 feet of air under your feet as you lunge for the next hold can provide a feeling that no other activity can. The satisfaction after grabbing the hold is unparalleled, too. Climbing demands complete focus on the task at hand, clearing the mind of daily distractions.

Although completing a climb is a solo accomplishment where your own power and decision making determine your success, climbing is an incredibly social activity. To climb on a rope, you need a partner to ensure your safety. To boulder without a rope near the ground, you often need spotters to help control your fall. Whatever the type of climbing, your partners can motivate you and make the activity more enjoyable. These bonds last far longer than the duration of your climb.

Climbing is an activity where elite performers and beginners can participate with each other. Everyone in the climbing gym has something in common: their appreciation of climbing.

For someone interested in rock climbing, starting with gym climbing is a logical first step. The technical skills of gym climbing are transferable to climbing outdoors. For a lot of people, climbing gyms are more accessible than outdoor climbing destinations. It may be impossible to go rock climbing after work or school, but a climbing gym allows for easy access and enjoyment. Another appeal of indoor climbing is the control of the environment. Devoid of bugs, rock fall, storms, sweltering heat, snow, or steep approaches, gyms provide a more comfortable environment for those who may be less inclined to pursue climbing outdoors.

HISTORY OF CLIMBING GYMS

Outdoor rock climbing is weather dependent. Sunny, warm days generally offer the best conditions, and the wetter and colder it is, the more dangerous the conditions. Even with perfect weather, you cannot rock climb without rock. So, climbers who just could not wait to climb on natural rock turned to alternate faces, like stone buildings or the underside of bridges.

Walls built specifically for climbing emerged in Europe. These basic outdoor structures resembled brick walls with holds chipped out and glued on pieces of rock. While these outdoor structures provided a great climbing opportunity on pleasant days, inclement weather rendered them useless. These walls were used by rock climbers who were looking for a way to train for climbing on stone. Outdoor walls are still popular in Europe. Most of the international climbing competitions are held at outdoor venues to allow for maximum spectator attendance.

In the late 1980s, indoor climbing walls became popular in the United States. Rather than mimic the real rock appearance of outdoor structures, hand holds were molded into more "tendon friendly" and comfortable shapes. This allowed climbers to train longer and to avoid injury. In addition, the indoor environment allowed climbers to train at any time of the day and in any season. The shift to climbing indoors also lowered the barrier of entry to the sport for beginning climbers. Now, there is a whole population of climbers who learned to climb indoors.

Today's indoor climbing walls are generally constructed with a steel frame covered by plywood and coated with a textured surface. There are some companies that build walls that look and even feel like real rock. These walls even have natural features that can be used as foot- and handholds. Almost all indoor walls have bolt-on climbing holds that are periodically moved around to create new routes.

WHERE TO FIND INDOOR CLIMBING

Because climbing gyms are so popular, it is possible to open up the Yellow Pages to find a list of climbing gyms. Climbing magazines also contain comprehensive lists. Finally, countless online gym listings are a great resource, particularly if you are traveling and want to get a climbing session in.

WHAT TO LOOK FOR IN A CLIMBING GYM

Most major cities offer some sort of gym-climbing facility, even those without local rock climbing areas. Florida, the flattest state, boasts at least nine gyms! If your gym-climbing options are limited, then you will simply climb at the nearest gym. If you are fortunate enough to have several options, not all gyms are created equal.

The most common question is how tall are the walls? This may seem like the most important issue for a new climber, but climbers have different needs in a gym. The novice climber may look for one with a reputation for offering great instructional classes. In contrast, an elite outdoor climber might look for a gym with great route setting, overhanging walls, and a fitness center for training purposes.

SIZE

There are a handful of climbing gyms with wall heights higher than 50 feet, but a majority of gym walls are between 25 and 50 feet. Less than 30 feet makes for short routes, but then again, take what you can get. Often, gym advertisements show the total amount of wall space expressed in square feet. However, this does not give you any information about the layout of the facility, how tall the walls are, or even how much of it is really climbable. Keep in mind that gyms with more than 15,000 square feet of climbing surface are considered huge by industry standards.

ROUTE SETTING

Climbing gyms have specific paths, or routes, that are established by a route setter. The holds on the wall are made of a plastic resin and have a bolt hole through the middle, allowing the route setter to reposition the holds. For the most part, the routes are set with specific movements in mind by the setter. On more difficult

climbs, intricate and complex movements are designed. Since route setters have their own distinct styles of setting, having more than one working for your climbing gym helps ensure some variety in the style of routes to climb. A well-rounded gym has a wide selection of routes, from easy ladderlike climbs for beginners and children to test pieces for elite climbers. Each route is rated in terms of difficulty, using the Yosemite Decimal System (YDS).

TOP-ROPING

When most people think of climbing, top-rope climbing usually comes to mind. With this style of climbing, the climber ties in to the end of a rope that is already attached to an anchor at the top of the climb and then runs back down to the belayer standing on the ground. The belayer is the climber's partner who minimizes the slack in the rope between the two of them as the climber ascends the wall. If the climber falls or wants to weight the rope, the belayer secures the rope to keep it from slipping. The belayer is also responsible for lowering the climber back to the ground. Top-roping is the most popular introduction to climbing.

LEAD CLIMBING

The limitation to top-roping outdoors is setting up an anchor at the top of the climb. If climbing a big rock wall or mountain, it is impossible to secure the first climber with a top-rope, since getting to the top is the adventure's objective! In these instances, the climber ascends with the rope trailing

Top-rope climbing is the most popular style of climbing. The climber is protected by a rope anchored from above.

down to the belayer. The belayer feeds rope out to the climber as he or she goes up. To protect the climber from hitting the ground after a fall, pieces of protective gear are placed into the rock and the rope is clipped to them. In the event of a fall, the climber falls past the last piece of protective gear until the rope is pulled taut. For safety reasons, climbing gyms use fixed bolts for lead climbers to clip the rope in to (also known as sport climbing). Lead climbing and belaying are the most technically (and mentally) demanding forms of gym climbing, since consequences of a fall are more serious than top-roping.

BOULDERING

A few decades ago, rock climbers scrambled over boulders to get to rock faces. Today, climbing on these refrigerator- to building–sized boulders is a sport in its own right. Bouldering is characterized as difficult unroped climbing, usually not very high off the ground, although some extremists push the envelope with high ascents. Boulderers protect themselves from high-speed impacts with the ground by landing on padded mats and using spotters, similar to gymnasts. Bigger climbing gyms have designated bouldering areas, without top-rope or lead climbs set above them.

Without the security of a top-rope, lead climbers face potentially longer falls.

Characterized as difficult movement near the ground, bouldering allows climbers to enjoy the freedom of unhindered movement without ropes and hardware.

INSTRUCTION

While instructional literature (like this book) is a reference for climbing skills and techniques, hands-on instruction from a qualified professional is essential for safety and continued progress. Sure, your buddy can "show you the ropes," but how do you know he is a competent and safe climber? Just because he is "a really good climber" does not mean he can verbalize the nuances of body positioning or advanced technical skills. Beginners are not the only group of climbers who can benefit from instruction. At any stage of your climbing career, there is always more to learn and an instructor can help advance your skills.

Indoor climbing schools vary greatly. Some have weekly classes and programs, while others only offer private instruction. If possible, get the "insider's feel" of the climbing school's classes by asking other climbers about their experiences. Find out where the class is held, since learning how to belay or boulder in a crowded area with climbers not in your class can be hectic and can detract from your learning. Ask the gym staff about the ratio of students per instructor, total number of students in the class, and frequency of classes to see what is right for you. More than six students per instructor for any type of climbing class are difficult to manage.

Find out what type of training the instructors receive before being able to teach classes. Surprisingly enough, there is no national certification for gym-climbing instructors, so any training will have been administered by the climbing school. The quality of an indoor climbing school is only as good as its instructors. Do not be afraid to ask for the best instructor to suit your needs, even for group classes.

NOT JUST CLIMBING

Climbing-gym owners are well aware that their member base is built of people who value the fitness and well-being that climbing provides. Many climbing gyms take their tie to health and fitness one step further by offering non-climbing-related services and facilities. It is common to see pieces of strength training or cardiovascular equipment in climbing gyms, and some even offer state-of-the-art fitness centers for their members. Yoga classes are gaining popularity in climbing centers, along with massage therapy and health-conscious cafés and coffee bars.

INDOOR CLIMBING IN FITNESS CENTERS

Just like climbing gyms are adding components of overall physical fitness and health to their facilities, fitness centers are adding climbing walls. Acknowledging the growing popularity of indoor climbing as a form of fitness, traditional gyms are taking steps like modifying racquetball courts to build climbing walls or adding treadmill-style climbing machines to satisfy their clients' desires to climb. Because climbing is not the primary focus of these establishments, you are better off seeking a commercial climbing gym to meet your needs. However, there are a few fitness centers that have more than adequate climbing facilities.

Community centers and organizations like the YMCA are also adding climbing walls to their facilities. Climbing promotes a healthy and active lifestyle particularly among youth and can even help improve self-confidence and body and spatial awareness. Perhaps the largest institutional push to building climbing walls is from colleges and universities. Newer recreation centers have climbing walls included in their designs, with older facilities adding artificial outdoor climbing walls. These walls are often a part of outdoor recreation programs.

Check on the availability of using climbing walls that are not in commercial climbing gyms. Some of these facilities allow climbers to use their walls with a daily fee, even if you are not a facility member.

YOUTH AND GYM CLIMBING

Gym climbers are all ages, but kids take to scaling the walls like monkeys take to trees. Children's small size and fearless attitudes make no climb too challenging to try. To accommodate the growing number of young climbers, most gyms have children-specific courses and programs. Climbing is so popular with kids that climbing birthday parties are common. Check for times that an instructor is available to belay for children. For kids who want more than just an opportunity to climb, look for youth programs that teach more advanced skills like belaying or climbing technique.

Kids view climbing facilities like an enormous jungle gym. They can never start too young!

Junior climbing teams have reached an all-time high, as most gyms support a youth climbing team. Not all teams share the same values, though. Some may have stringent training schedules planned around the spring competition season, with intensity similar to gymnastics. Others teams simply create an environment to allow youth to climb with each other on a regular basis with little focus on competition.

WHAT TO EXPECT

GETTING STARTED

If you are new to climbing, your gym may have options for you to get started. If you have never climbed or belayed before, few gyms are set up to allow you to try climbing or receive instruction on a walk-in basis. If a gym has auto-belay systems (mechanical belay systems that do not require a belayer), they may be able to let you climb at any time. Check into open climbing times, during which an instructor is available to let you try a few climbs for a nominal fee. While noninstructional programs can get you climbing, an introductory class gives you a better feel for the activity as a whole.

TAKING AN INTRODUCTORY CLASS

Climbing for the first time requires little instruction, but belaying requires a certain level of competence and a learned set of skills. Enrolling in an introductory class is the best way to start your climbing career. Usually, an introductory class is several hours long and teaches how to properly put on a safety harness, tie in to the rope as a climber, and belay, all while allowing for some time to climb. These skills are essential to any type of roped climbing you may pursue, indoors or outside. Climbing shoes, a harness, and belay hardware should be included with the class. Be wary of classes that last less than an hour, since retaining belay skills comes from repeated practice. The responsibilities of a belayer are serious, with potentially extreme consequences for mistakes. An introductory class prepares you to take (and hopefully pass) a belay competency test. Some gyms have packages that include an introductory course and limited free entry to the facility.

BELAY TEST

Before a gym allows you to belay unsupervised, you must take and pass a belay test. This "practical exam" shows the gym staff that you know the basic principles of how to use a harness, belay, and can properly tie in to the rope as a climber. There is no set standard for this test, but following the techniques and procedures in this book will adequately prepare you for any belay test. Some gyms administer rather stringent belay tests, while others give them in passing. Since each gym sets its own standards, there is no national belay-test certification. For every gym you climb at, you will have to take their belay test. Gyms test climbers for top-rope climbing and lead climbing separately, and all gyms have a minimum age requirement for belay testing.

WAIVER OF LIABILITY

Every gym requires participants to sign a waiver of liability before climbing or belaying. The most common public perception is that this waiver's sole purpose is to avoid litigation should an accident occur. But more importantly, signing the waiver acknowledges risk on behalf of the participant. It is in your best interest to read every word of the waiver, especially first-time climbers. Some gyms even have you sign a helmet waiver if you choose to not wear a helmet.

Climbing, just like driving your car or mountain biking, entails risk. Your climbing gym has created an opportunity for you to climb, and your gym has therefore also created a risk to you. Signing the waiver means that you understand and are aware of these risks and *choose* to cling to a wall 30 feet up in the air. Ultimately, you are responsible for your own actions and safety. Think twice about climbing gyms that do not require waivers or belay tests. Such actions are evidence that the gym does not take reasonable precautions to help create a safe climbing environment.

ENTRY OPTIONS

On average, expect to pay $10 to $16 for a day pass. Off-peak hours may be cheaper, like during a weekday afternoon. A day pass should allow you to leave and reenter the gym and is usually the only option for a day of climbing, regardless of how long you climb. Rental fees are in addition to the entry fee. Shoes, harness, and belay equipment normally rent for $10 all

together. Most gyms offer bulk-rate day passes, like a punch card, or multiple visits at a cheaper rate. Monthly passes are a nice option if you are going to climb at a gym over the summer or winter.

Gym memberships are usually the way to go if you plan to climb at least once a week (climbing two or three times a week is common for gym climbers). Ranging anywhere from $35 to $75 a month, these memberships are similar to a fitness center membership. This fee allows you to climb whenever the gym is open and may even give you extra perks such as free courses, guest passes, members' parties, or even gear or instruction discounts.

CHAPTER 2

Equipment

A love of climbing comes from the freedom of moving in a vertical environment. However, this freedom can position us 40 feet off the ground and in potentially dangerous situations. Climbing gear is the link between safety and pushing your physical and mental limits. Rope attaches the climber and belayer to each other, harnesses attach the rope to the climber and the belayer, and carabiners attach the rope to the harnesses. Not only does this gear minimize the risk of injury, but it also enhances performance and makes climbing more enjoyable. Neither climbing shoes nor chalk is essential for gym-climbing safety, but both can make climbing more enjoyable.

PURCHASING EQUIPMENT

You trust your life to the gear you purchase and use. With this in mind, make sure that everything properly fits and functions. Try on all your equipment and get an expert opinion on its fit. Try to fit your gear at the same place you will purchase it. Where you purchase your climbing gear can affect how well it is fitted to you.

Due to the importance of safety for climbing gear, most retailers do not take returns on safety equipment (carabiners, harnesses, etc.), even if the product is unused. This further emphasizes the importance of proper fit before making purchases. Exchanges under warrantee may be brought back to the retailer, but in some cases you must deal directly with the manufacturer.

MAIL ORDER/WEBSITES

Mail order and website stores have gained popularity with their discount prices and ease of purchasing. However, you cannot try the gear on and in-person customer service obviously is not available. Purchasing an item that you have already owned or tried on is appropriate. You can find excellent close-out or overstock deals on climbing gear through websites and mail order. However, if a retail store provides you with customer service, they deserve your patronage.

OUTDOOR AND SPORTING GOODS STORES

Sporting goods stores that have climbing departments generally offer the smallest selection of gear and the least-experienced staff. Outdoor stores are a better bet for well-stocked climbing departments and knowledgeable staff. Since employees may be assigned to different departments, ask for a climbing specialist. Do not work with someone who knows less than you do.

CLIMBING-SPECIFIC STORES

Climbing-specific retailers are an excellent source of climbing gear. Usually located near outdoor climbing destinations, these shops hire climbers who have practical experience with the gear they sell. Most likely, a small climbing wall is available to fit test gear before purchasing. The selection is usually up to date with the latest gear innovations.

CLIMBING GYMS

A majority of climbing gyms have some sort of retail shop, although the selection of gear varies widely. Often, larger climbing gyms have a greater retail selection. As a gym climber, it makes sense to seek information about, get fitted, and purchase gear from the same people that you will see in the gym on a regular basis.

Climbing gyms are often the site of gear

demonstrations, or demos. Depending on the gym, climbing-gear representatives (often from shoe and harness companies) bring in products for climbers to try out on the wall. This is the most effective way to try out gear and decide what you like. With a manufacturer's representative present, you can find the perfect fit and get answers to any technical questions. Ask your climbing gym about the frequency of gear demos.

USED GEAR

Purchasing used gear is not recommended for safety equipment. It is important to know the clear, firsthand history of nylon items and hardware. Nylon items (like a harness) that have been exposed to harmful solvents (like battery acid or bleach) should not be used, even if they pass a visual inspection. Carabiners and belay devices may look new, but having been dropped from even a nominal height can affect the integrity of their strength.

Purchasing used climbing shoes is not so much of a safety issue, so make your own decisions on their value and condition. Online auction sites sell plenty of used gear, and most climbing gyms have bulletin boards with postings for used gear. Purchasing used shoes for children whose feet are still growing is an economical move for parents.

GEAR STANDARDS AND TESTING

The Union Internationale des Associations d'Alpinisme (UIAA) is a governing body that sets safety standards of climbing gear. Their laboratory tests set minimum standards for safety equipment such as ropes, sewn nylon products (like webbing and harnesses), carabiners, and belay devices. Climbing-gear companies conduct their own tests for product development and safety measures, usually (but not always) to UIAA guidelines. In general, gym climbing gear available for purchase at established climbing retailers meets or exceeds UIAA standards. Do not take your own safety for granted though. For more information on the technical specifications of particular equipment, contact the manufacturer.

THE ESSENTIAL ITEMS

HARNESS

When climbing with ropes, a harness is essential for safety and comfort. It is the attachment point between your body and the rope. The main differences in harnesses are adjustability, padding, materials, weight, and fit. An improperly fitting harness is not only uncomfortable, but potentially dangerous, as well.

The most popular type of harness consists of a waist belt, leg loops, and a belay loop. Purchased in different sizes according to waist and leg circumference, these harnesses fit a wide range of body types. Full-body chest harnesses are appropriate for children too small to fit in a waist-belt harness, but are not suitable for adults. Although difficult to correctly tie and uncomfortable, it is possible to make

A harness with adjustable leg loops

Some harnesses have self-locking buckles that are always secure. With two waist-belt buckles, the middle of this harness will always line up with the climber's front and back.

your own harness with tubular webbing, but climbing gyms only allow commercially manufactured harnesses in their facilities.

Waist Belt

The most comfortable harnesses have thick padding and wide webbing to disperse the climber's weight. Thoughtfully designed harnesses are wider across the back, where more pressure is created when the harness is weighted, and tapered toward the front to minimize bulk. Various types and layers of foam laid into the core of the waist belt provide padding. Synthetic lining on the inside can add comfort against the skin. Some companies use mesh fabrics or open cutouts in the back of the harness to keep the climber cooler in warm weather.

Harnesses have one or two buckles on the waist belt. One buckle makes the harness slightly lighter (and cheaper). However, if a climber is in between waist-belt sizes, a harness with a single-buckle waist belt may mean that the center of the waist belt's back might not line up with the center of the climber's back. With two-buckle waist belts, tightening each buckle evenly allows the front and back of the waist belt to stay centered on the climber.

Buckles

At a minimum, a harness will have one buckle on the waist belt. Some may have up to four buckles (two on the waist belt and one on each leg). Keep in mind that multiple buckles add minor weight and bulk to your harness. Regardless of how many buckles the harness has and where

Non-self-locking buckles must be doubled-backed before using. To make sure the buckle is secure, only half of the buckle should be visible, with the other side covered by the threaded piece of webbing. Make sure at least 4 inches of tail is left over.

they are located, they must be securely locked before use. A few manufacturers use self-locking buckles, but the standard buckle must be manually doubled-backed for security.

Leg Loops

Similarly constructed to the waist belt, padding and width contribute to the leg loops' comfort. A harness will either have fixed leg loops or adjustable leg loops. Fixed leg loops are proportionally sized to the waist belt. If you have a narrow waist and sturdy thighs, the buckles on adjustable leg loops allow for a wide range of leg size. This is helpful for a comfortable fit when layering with pants or shorts, depending on the environment.

Belay Loop

The belay loop is a reinforced loop of webbing that attaches the waist belt to the leg loops. The strongest part of the harness, the belay loop is the connection point to the belay device and floor anchors.

Gear Loops

Only cheap, entry-level or rental harnesses do not have gear loops. Harnesses appropriate for gym climbing should have at least one gear loop on each side. When climbing, your belay device and carabiners hang from the gear loops, rather than dangling from your belay loop. Four gear loops is common, but harnesses with up to six are designed for carrying the vast amounts of equipment needed for outdoor leading. Gear is more easily unclipped from plastic molded rigid loops than from webbing surrounded by plastic tubing.

Rear Keeper Straps

The rear keeper straps attach the back of the leg loops to the back of the waist belt. Tightening these straps keeps the leg loops high on the thigh. Loose straps let the leg

UNIVERSITY OF CENTRAL LANCASHIRE LIBRARY

loops sag uncomfortably and limit range of leg motion. Detachable straps can be helpful in outdoor climbing, but are not necessary indoors.

Harness Fit

Waist. When fitting your harness, compare your waist size to the manufacturer's sizing chart. This will give you a good indication of where to start. Stepping through the leg loops, pull them up as high as comfortable on your thighs. Thread the waist buckle(s) with the webbing and pull the waist belt snug around the smallest part of your waist above your hips. (The webbing of an autolocking slide buckle is already threaded.) The waist belt must be tight enough that if you were to flip over, the harness would still be secure. Once the waist belt is tight, the belay loop should line up with your navel, and the middle of the back of the harness should line up with the middle of your back.

Legs. The leg loops should fit snugly around your upper thighs, but without interfering with movement. You should be able to comfortably slip two fingers between the leg loop and your thigh. If the waist belt fits properly but the leg loops do not, consider a harness with adjustable leg loops. Properly sized leg loops can still slide down your thigh, so tighten the rear keeper straps to minimize droopy leg loops.

Rise. Although waist-belt and leg-loop size is important, the distance of the waist belt from the leg loops should not be overlooked. This distance is the rise of the harness. Although there is no sizing for a harness's rise, test fitting is the best indication for proper length. More often, the harness's rise is too short than too long. A short rise creates a pull between the leg loops and the waist belt. This constant pull can be uncomfortable and may compromise the fit and function of the harness. In general, women need a longer rise and woman-specific harnesses compensate for the gender difference. There are a few harness models with an adjustable rise, helping create the perfect fit.

Weighed fit. When standing on the ground, just about every properly fitting harness is comfortable. However, the true test of fit is while hanging. Your climbing gear retailer should have a test rope. Make sure that you clip or tie in to both the leg loop connector strap and the waist belt.

While hanging in the harness, pay attention to the distribution of pressure created by the waist belt and leg loops. It should be fairly even; this distribution of weight is a function of the harness's rise. A different rise may improve fit. Acute pressure on your lower back, sides of your waist, and legs depends on the padding, width, and shaping of the materials. Avoid any painful biting or pinching in these areas. Only after a weighted test should you make the decision to purchase a harness. The most expensive harness is not going to help you climb any better, so seek the best fitting one.

Caring for Soft Gear

Harnesses and all other soft climbing gear are made of nylon. While light and strong, nylon is susceptible to chemical and ultraviolet light damage. Keep your nylon gear away from chemicals or other acidic substances (even cat urine!). If in contact with questionable substances, retire the gear. If cleaning your gear to get rid of dirt or sweat, use a soft brush and a gentle soap or detergent without bleach. Rinse several times with cool, clean water and lay your gear to dry in a cool environment out of direct sunlight. Store your gear in a cool, dry place (not the trunk of your car in the summer) to prevent molding.

CLIMBING SHOES

While a harness is the most important piece of safety gear that requires fitting, it minimally affects climbing performance. Shoes, however, while not essential to climbing safety, are the single most important piece of equipment affecting how you climb. Throughout climbing's history, technological shoe advances have significantly affected the evolution of rock climbing. With their sticky rubber and secure fit, they will make a difference in your climbing, too.

Last

Climbing shoes are constructed on either a board last or a slip last. The last is the constructed inner sole of the shoe. A board-lasted shoe is made by using a board as the base sole of the shoe and building the rest of the shoe around it. The end result is a shoe that is extremely stiff and durable. This is beneficial for rock climbing and crack climbing, but the lack of

sensitivity is less than desirable for gym climbing. There are only a few board-lasted shoes on the market and you probably will not find them in your climbing gym's retail shop.

All gym climbing and multipurpose rock-climbing shoes are constructed on a slip last. With this style, the shoe is constructed and then a last is slipped into the sole. The sensitivity of slip-lasted shoes is determined by the thickness and material of the midsole and the thickness of the shoe rubber. Slip-lasted shoes are the choice of the indoor climber.

Shape

The shape of the last is the shoe's "footprint" and contributes to overall fit and comfort. A straight last creates minimal torque on the foot and is the most comfortable. New climbers and someone wanting a shoe to wear all day will find a straight last desirable. The more curved the last, the more pressure and torque on the foot. This is helpful with high-performance climbing on steep and technical terrain, as the toes are more down-pointed.

Rubber

No two climbing-shoe manufacturers use the same rubber compounds on their shoes. The differences are stickiness and durability. Softer rubbers tend to be stickier, but wear more quickly than harder, less sticky compounds. Some climbers may go through a lifetime of climbing and not be able to tell the difference between rubbers, while others swear by one brand over

A selection of rock climbing shoes suitable for gym and outdoor use. From the left, the Venom is a sensitive slipper with a mesh rubber toe cover. The Testarossa is a lace-up model designed for maximum toe power and a precise fit. The Velcro shoe, Katana, has a synthetic and leather upper. The last shoe is the Lady Mythos, designed with a higher arch and narrower heel for women. All the shoes are slip-lasted and made by La Sportiva.

another and even have brand-new shoes resoled with the rubber of their choice. Most shoes are constructed with 4–5mm rubber soles, while high-performance shoes use rubber as thin as 3mm for sensitivity. Shoes with thin rubber wear out faster than thicker soles.

Upper Material

The upper part of the shoe is either made from leather or synthetic materials. Leather is typically cheaper, stretches from prolonged use, and is highly durable. Synthetic uppers offer a soft, thin feel, while minimizing stretch and maintaining durability. Most climbing-shoe manufacturers offer shoe models of leather or synthetic uppers. Some shoes may have a combination of both materials. For instance, a synthetic toe box keeps the fit tight around the toes but leather around the rest of the shoe opening provides a comfortable fit.

Lining

The shoe's upper material and lining (or lack of lining) determines the overall stretch of the shoe. The lining is often a canvas or synthetic material on the inside of the shoe. Lining a shoe can maximize comfort and feel while minimizing stretch. The stretch of an unlined shoe is at the mercy of the upper materials. An unlined synthetic upper may stretch as little as a lined leather upper. Unlined leather shoes stretch the most, as much as a full size after persistent use.

Style

There are three general styles of climbing shoes: slippers, Velcro, and lace-ups. They all have their place in climbing and some styles are more appropriate than others, depending on the terrain.

Slippers. Slippers are constructed without laces or a closure system. An extremely tight fit and elastic at the opening keep the shoe secure on the foot. However, once the shoe is on, fit adjustments are impossible. If there are any loose spots in the shoe, the only way to tighten them is by wearing a smaller shoe. Because of the extremely tight fit, most climbers wear their slippers only while climbing and take them off while belaying or resting. The midsole of slippers is thin and soft (even nonexistent in some models), allowing maximum sensitivity. On steep terrain, you can actually curl the toes around footholds for maximum feel with a soft slipper. This benefits experienced climbers who have developed the proper foot strength to use their feet efficiently. Because of their minimalist construction, slippers are priced at the lower end of the spectrum. However, inefficient footwork can quickly grind down the rubber and ruin a new pair of slippers within months.

Velcro. Velcro-closure shoes are a great compromise between the speed and ease of putting on a slipper and the support and fit of a lace-up shoe. The Velcro closure straps make putting on the shoes a breeze and provide some fit adjustment once they are on. Within Velcro style shoes, some are extremely sensitive and soft while others have more edging power. Some companies offer zipper-closure shoes instead of Velcro. Velcro-closure shoes are popular among gym and sport climbers because they blend sensitivity with fit and performance.

Lace-up. Lace-up climbing shoes offer the most adjustability in fit. The lacing system extends all the way down to the toes, providing adjustment points through-out the entire shoe. Tightening or loosening the laces at different spots on the shoe provides the most exact fit of all the shoe styles. For the most part, lace-up shoes offer greater foot stability and a strong edging platform, imperative for small edges. Entry-level lace-ups are constructed to provide foot support and stability, as well as durability. For all-around climbing on varying terrain, lace-ups are an excellent option when buying your first shoe.

Trying Shoes On

While research may help you narrow your choice of shoes down to a selected few, the most important criteria is fit. If possible, buy the actual shoe that you have tried on. Because of the handmade craftsmanship, there can be slight differences in fit, even with the same size shoe of the same model. Trying on shoes can be a tiresome process, but patience will get you the most out of your investment.

Climbing shoes are usually worn without socks. Wearing socks creates another barrier between your feet and the wall. This additional barrier makes your foot slide and move around while climbing and hinders sensitivity.

To get your foot into the shoe, open the shoes up as much as possible. For slippers, fold the heel down to the sole to maximize the opening. Slide your foot all the way to the front of the shoe and use the heel tabs to slip the back of the shoe over your heel. For lace-ups, loosen the laces all the way down to the toe. Tighten the laces starting with the toes and work your way up to the ankle.

There is no adjusting with slippers, and Velcro shoes offer minimal adjustments.

Shoe Fit

Climbing shoes should fit snugly, but should not be overly tight or painful. Your toes should be at the end of the shoe with not much wiggle room. A snug fit alleviates sliding inside the shoe and allows for more precise footwork. However, if the shoes are painful, your attention will be focused on your feet, not the climbing. Look for an all-around snug fit but avoid pressure points or loose spots. Also, excessive bunching of the upper material should be avoided. Your heel should be cradled by the shoe with limited dead space. In your search for a new shoe, take your time and be sure to try on shoes from different manufacturers. Some companies have reputations of fitting certain types of feet, but give several shoes a try.

The type of shoe also influences the fit. A slipper with a down-turned toe and radically curved last warrants a tight fit, with the knuckles of the toes buckled up and toe tips scrunched into the end of the shoe. A straight-lasted lace-up with a flat-foot design allows the toes to lay flat and just barely touch the front of the shoe. Wearing a loose slipper or the lace-up too tight limits the functionality of the shoe.

Consider the shoe's potential stretch. As mentioned before, this is dependent on the upper material, lining, and shoe size. Whoever is helping you fit your shoes should be able to tell you how much a shoe stretches. The tighter a shoe fits, the more pressure is created on the uppers and the stretch potential increases.

Like fitting a harness, a wall test is your best indicator of performance and fit. Your climbing-gear retailer should allow you to step on some holds to get a feel for the shoes. If that is not possible, stand up and down on the edge of a bench or step to imitate climbing footwork and placement. Also, try to pull the shoe off of your foot by hooking your heel on a hold or edge. The shoe should still be secure under this heel hook test.

Once you find the best-fitting shoe, take one more step to ensure it is the perfect-fitting shoe. Try on the next size up and down so you know the size you choose is best suited for you.

All these steps are necessary in buying shoes since they are not returnable once climbed in and you do not want to be stuck with ill-fitting footwear. Use a climbing-shoe expert for advice and guidance, but ultimately the choice is yours. If you are uncertain about the sizing, you can always add socks to shoes that stretch too much to make them wearable, but if the shoes are too small, they are useless.

Caring for Shoes

Wearing tight-fitting and nonbreathable shoes without socks and walking around barefoot before putting them on is less than hygienic. Do not be the one your friends avoid when you pull your shoes out of your bag. Zap your shoes with antibacterial spray or powder after a climbing session and store them outside your bag so they can ventilate.

Once again, the hot trunk of your car is not a good place for climbing gear.

If the insides of the shoes turn black from who knows what (it does happen), scrub them with a bit of mild detergent or soap, using a small brush. For the soles, avoid walking in dirt and dust. This is not a problem in padded gyms, but when pea gravel is the flooring, consider wearing sandals. The rubbing pea gravel creates dust that imbeds in the rubber, making the soles less sticky. Clear the soles by scrubbing them with a wire brush and rubbing alcohol. Periodically check the soles for excessive wear.

Resoling

Eventually, the soles of climbing shoes wear down, usually near the inside edge. It is simply a matter of when, not if. A climber of delicate and precise footwork may get a year of climbing without needing a resole. Shoes of someone who uses "aggressive" footwork (loud foot placements and scraping or dragging the toes against the wall) may need doctoring after only a few months. Resoling saves your shoes and keeps you from having to purchase another pair, and there are multiple mail-in climbing shoe resolers.

A brand-new pair of climbing shoes has an even seam where the sole of the shoe meets the thin rubber that comes up from the bottom on the sides and front (the rand). When this seam becomes jagged near the toe, or the sole starts to delaminate from the rand, send the shoes in for a half resole. The cobbler will replace that half of the sole

This shoe is ready for a resole. If worn much longer, the rand will wear through.

with new rubber. The work of a skilled resoler will not affect the sizing or shape of your shoe. If you wait longer before resoling your shoes and wear into or through the toe rand, then a half sole and re-rand operation is necessary for resuscitation. Having a shoe re-randed often changes the shape of the toe box and if a hole wears past the rand to the leather, you are too late.

CARABINERS

Carabiners are literal links that a climber uses to attach pieces of gear, webbing, and ropes. They are a closed ring of aluminum alloy or steel that open with a spring-loaded gate to keep the carabiner closed. There are several carabiner body types, gates, and closures.

Nonlocking Gates

Nonlocking carabiners are used for attaching rope or gear together. They are easy to manipulate and open with ease. However, easy opening has its drawbacks, especially when you want the gate closed. Clipping-end carabiners on lead climbs in the gym are nonlocking.

Carabiners with straight gates are standard multifunction carabiners, while bent gates make clipping the rope with one hand much easier. Wire gates reduce the overall weight of the carabiner, and their decreased mass over conventional gates make then less likely to open from vibration.

Locking Gates

Locking carabiners provide more security at integral attachment points. An anchor carabiner or one used with a belay device should be secured with a locking mechanism. The most common locking mechanism is the screw lock, where a sleeve manually screws down to cover the carabiner gate and body, keeping it from opening. Common sense would have you screw down the locking sleeve until tight, but after a force weights the carabiner, the sleeve will further tighten. You may find yourself with a gate sleeve that will not unlock in that case. So, once the gate sleeve reaches its locking point, loosen the

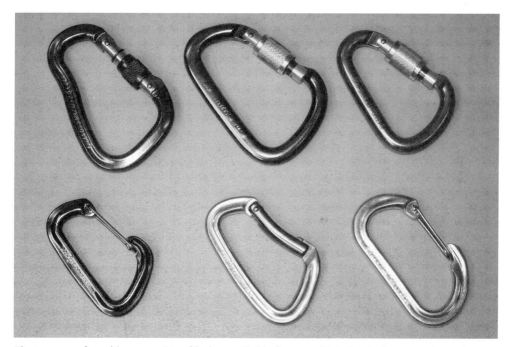

The top row of carabiners consists of lockers, suitable for use with belay devices or anchor points. On the bottom are nonlocking carabiners with wire and bent gates to make clipping the rope with one hand easier.

sleeve about a quarter turn. The gate will still be locked, but the sleeve will be loose enough to unscrew.

Autolocking and button-locking carabiners are alternatives to screw-lock gates. To open these gates, the user must either first rotate the locking sleeve or hold down a button while opening the carabiner. Personal preference and ease of opening are the deciding factors in which type of locking carabiner you use.

Shape

There are different carabiner body designs for many applications. Originally, all carabiners were symmetrically oval. From the oval design came the D-shaped carabiner, which puts more of the carabiner's load on the spine, increasing the carabiner's strength. Most carabiners used today are a modified offset D shape. The modification creates a wide end on one side and a narrow end on the other, maximizing the carabiner's strength-to-weight ratio.

The smooth action of symmetrically shaped pear carabiners makes them a popular choice with tubular belay devices.

Strength

Carabiners are remarkably strong for their size and weight. However, the position of pull makes a difference in breaking strength. Designed to be pulled along the axis of the spine with the gate closed, this orientation of pull offers the greatest strength of about 5000 pounds of force. An open gate greatly compromises strength, holding only 1500 to 2000 pounds of force

A carabiner is designed to be pulled along the spine as shown: prevent loads from running in any other direction.

before failure. Cross-loading a carabiner by pulling across the spine and gate holds even less weight. Take care to ensure that the direction of pull on any carabiner is along the spine.

BELAY DEVICES

The belayer uses a belay device to help hold the climber in the event of a fall and to smoothly lower the climber in a controlled manner. The device attaches to the belayer's harness and to the climbing rope running through it, creating enough friction to allow the belayer to control the rope manually. For rock climbing, most belay devices can be used for rappelling or for descending a fixed rope, but these actions are not necessary in gym climbing. It is possible to belay without a belay device, but these techniques are less secure and climbing gyms require the use of a UIAA-approved device.

Tubular Belay Devices

Tubular belay devices have a stronghold on climbers as a popular belay device. A loop of rope is pushed into the device and clipped with a locking carabiner. Rope feeds through the belay device and in the event of a fall, the series of bends in the rope through the device create enough friction to hold the impact of the fall. The belayer simply holds the rope in the appropriate orientation to allow for maximum friction. Tubular belay devices are popular for their versatility as a rappel device, their low cost, and their light weight.

There are many variations of the tubular device, all working on the same principles. Gaining popularity are grooved devices with teeth, where the brake strand runs over the side of the device. These grooves increase the amount of surface area between the rope and device, thus creating more friction and increasing holding power.

Petzl GriGri

The Petzl GriGri is a belay device that uses a self-braking system. Larger, heavier, and more costly than a tubular device, the GriGri's locking mechanism works like a seatbelt. In the event of a fall, the quick

Tubular belay devices are popular because of their easy use, light weight, and low cost. The Petzl GriGri (center) has been embraced by gym climbers because of its self-braking mechanism.

rope movement cams the locking device down on the rope, pinching it in place. A lever releases the pinch and controls the climber's descent. GriGris are very popular with gym climbers.

Caring for Hardware

Metal climbing hardware (like carabiners and belay devices) are susceptible to invisible hairline factures if dropped onto hard surfaces. Since padding covers most gym-climbing floors, such damage is not a problem indoors. Still, develop a healthy respect for your gear.

Over time, the moving parts of your hardware (like the gate hinges or locking sleeves of carabiners) can become caked with dirt and affect the piece's mechanics. Applying a lubricant such as WD-40 will loosen the grime and keep the parts moving freely. Also give your gear some tender loving care by identifying it with tape or some other marking that does not structurally affect the metal. It is easy to mix up equipment with other climbers in the gym since gear choices are limited.

ROPE

The rope is the lifeline between the climber and belayer and is engineered to climbing's impact demands. While it is important to understand how a climbing rope works to improve your safety, the decision of what model or diameter rope used in your gym is probably already made for you. Whether you are lead climbing or top-roping, the gym provides the ropes. This way, they can inspect and replace the ropes at regular intervals and manage the number of people climbing routes at a given time.

The dynamic properties of climbing ropes allow them to elongate with the force of a fall. Imagine how uncomfortable (and dangerous) it would feel to take even a short fall with steel cable attached to your waist. Although not as elastic as a bungee cord, climbing-rope stretch increases the time it takes for the climber to stop. The longer it takes to slow the fall, the less force is created on the climber and the rest of the anchor system. The amount of stretch is also proportional to the amount of rope stretching. For example, falling at the bottom of a 40-foot top-rope (there would be approximately 80 feet of rope between the climber and belayer because the rope travels from the belayer to the top anchors and back down to the climber) creates more rope stretch than falling at the top of the same climb (now, only slightly more than 40 feet of rope connects the climber to the belayer). Keep this in mind when starting a top-roped climb. New ropes elongate much further than used ones, and smaller diameter ropes stretch more than thicker ropes.

A climbing rope is constructed with an inner core and an outer sheath. The dynamic properties of the rope are in the core, comprised of nylon filaments twisted together that stretch under the impact of a fall, and then slowly contract. The outer sheath is merely the protective casing for the core. Although not needed in the gym, you can buy a rope with a dry treatment for inclement weather. The sheath, core, or sometimes both receive a chemical treatment that prevents the rope from absorbing water. More pliable ropes have a looser sheath braid, giving them a nice feel but compromising the rope's protective qualities. More durable ropes have tight, thickly woven sheaths with a stiffer feel. Together, the core and sheath create a diameter of between 9mm and 11mm for a single climbing rope. With the high climbing traffic in gyms, expect to use a 10–11mm diameter rope with a durable sheath.

Although you do not own the rope you use in a climbing gym, treat it with care, since you trust your life to it. Stepping on the rope pushes dirt and dust into it, potentially compromising its longevity. When walking with a rope, pick it up, rather than dragging it across the floor.

GEAR CONSIDERATIONS

CHALK

Just as gymnasts use chalk to dry their hands and improve their grip, climbers do the same. The simplest form of chalk is carbonate magnesium, which comes in blocks to be crushed by the user. Powdered blends of chalk specifically designed for climbing are offered by several companies. These compounds have drying agents, but can cause excessive hand dryness for some users. Because loose chalk can create a white haze and less than desirable air quality without sufficient ventilation, some gyms do not allow it. The alternative is a chalk ball, which is a thin "sock" packed with chalk. Grabbing the ball slightly powders the hand, and it is refillable. Chalk is predominately white in color, but there are some environmentally friendly colors like brown and tan for outdoor use.

CHALK BAG

Chalk bags are hung in the middle of the back attached directly to the harness or its own belt. There are some minor differences in the function of a chalk bag. Look for one that is fully lined with fleece. This lining absorbs chalk and makes it easier to get your hands covered. Of course, make sure your hand fits into the bag. Chalk bags have a cinch strap to keep it closed when not in use. A chalk bag that closes securely will keep your climbing pack from a constant dusting of chalk. Since chalk bags come in so many different patterns, colors, and fabrics (you can even have them custom made), they are the only climbing accessory you can match to your personality!

BELAY GLOVES

If your hands are sensitive to holding the rope while belaying and lowering a climber, consider specially designed belay gloves. These gloves have a snug fit and a thin leather palm to provide protection from the rope running through the belayer's hands. This can build confidence in the belayer's ability to hold and lower a climber. Gloves also keep the belayer's hands clean from residue that comes off the rope. Before using belay gloves, consider using a different belay device that may provide more holding power, since

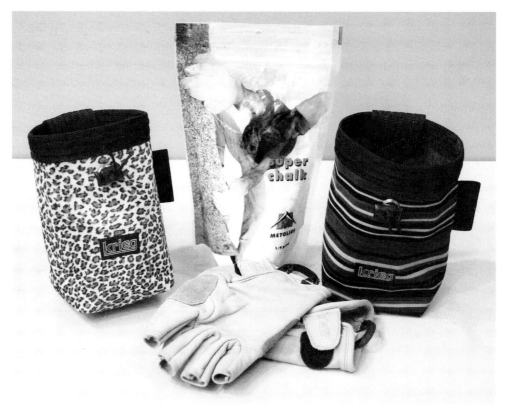

Chalk and a chalk bag can help keep your hands dry and improve grip on greased up holds. Consider using belay gloves for skin protection.

gloves decrease the belayer's sensitivity to the rope.

HELMET

While climbing outdoors, wearing a helmet is a safe practice. Helmets protect climbers from rocks and other falling objects. In the gym, however, helmets are seldom worn since falling objects are less likely than in outdoor rock climbing (carabiners can still fall, though). New climbers and young children should wear a helmet to protect their head if bumped against the wall if they lose their balance. Traditional climbing-specific helmets are constructed with a hard plastic, designed to take repeated abuse. Newer helmets with softer shells are lighter and more breathable, but are less durable and require greater care.

CLOTHING

Like any other activity or sport, climbing has its own activity-specific clothing. However, the leopard print climbing tights of the late 1980s are extinct and designers have moved to a more functional blend with popular fashion. Current fabrics are durable yet soft, and stretchy materials allow for unhindered movement and a maximum range of motion. Wicking fabrics help keep climbers cool, too. Shirts and pullovers are cut trim at the waist to easily fit under a harness, and fitted sleeves stay out of the way of grabbing holds. Pants or long shorts can protect the knees from scrapes and bruises, while tapered legs improve visibility of the feet for precise footwork. A bulky waistband on pants can be uncomfortable with a harness, so climb in something with a low-profile waist. However, the specific garments are not a necessity and any clothes that serve the mentioned functions are fine.

CHAPTER 3

Top-rope Climbing

Top-rope climbing is the first step in any climber's progression. Although the minimal gear of bouldering may appeal to the beginning climber, top-rope climbing develops the movement foundation that bouldering builds upon.

Top-rope climbs in a gym are set up as slingshot systems. The climber ties in to one end of the rope with it traveling up to an anchor and then back down to the belayer positioned on the ground. The belayer takes in rope as the climber ascends and keeps the rope from moving in the event of a fall. When the climber is ready to lower from the route, which can be done at any time or point, the belayer allows rope to slide through the belay device and controls the climber's speed of descent. Because the belayer is in control of all the rope work, the climber can focus on scaling the wall. Since the belayer needs to understand (and sometimes anticipate) the needs of the climber, a new student should start with climbing instruction before moving to belay instruction.

GRADE

Starting out on a route, most climbers tackle whatever looks fun to them, grabbing any and all holds available to get to the top. This type of climbing hooks novices back into the gym, but there is more to climbing than just conquering the wall and getting to the top. After a few climbs of grabbing any hold available, understanding the grading scale can direct the climber's attention to what routes are of a challenging grade.

Climbs are rated on the Yosemite Decimal System (YDS), a subjective scale of difficulty. Roped climbs are considered fifth class climbs. This means that without a rope, a fall from the route while climbing can be fatal. The other categories, first class through fourth class, refer to outdoor terrain ranging from hiking to scrambling with the hands and feet with or without a rope.

A gym route rating may or may not have the prefix 5, but will always include another set of numbers, and perhaps letters or a plus or minus. The numbers following "5." represent the difficulty of the route. The scale is open ended, but it starts at 1 and currently reaches 15. For grades above 10, the difficulty beaks down further in ascending order from a through d. For example, a 5.11b would be read "five eleven b" and would be slightly more difficult than a 5.11a. Sometimes a plus or minus is used instead of the letter rating.

Novice climbers usually start in the 5.5 to 5.7 range. Climbing 5.12 and beyond is a considerable accomplishment, requiring a strong command of climbing technique, physical conditioning, and mental resolve.

Several factors contribute to the subjective grade of a climb. The wall's terrain and the size, number, and spacing of the holds all affect the overall grade. In the gym, route setters create climbs based on their own experiences with rock climbing. Hard routes do not simply have fewer or smaller holds, but force the climber to use specific techniques. In fact, larger holds without a solid edge to grab are the most difficult to hold onto. Keep in mind that routes requiring long reaches for a short climber may be easier for a tall climber, and someone with smaller hands may find a climb easier (or harder) than someone with bigger hands.

Terrain, defined as the angle steepness of the climbing surface, plays a significant role in the difficulty of the route. A less than vertical wall, or slab, leans away from you while facing it. With slabby (less than vertical) terrain, you can keep your center of gravity over your feet and use your hands for balance, similar to walking up stairs. This is a good place to start for novice climbers, since the upper body does not become as fatigued as in vertical or steep climbing. Vertical and near-vertical climbs are straight up and down, forcing the climber to engage the arms more than on a less than vertical wall. The most impressive climbs to watch (and climb) are on steep, overhanging walls. The difficulty of steep terrain lies in the advanced techniques necessary to keep the climber's weight over the feet and not have the upper body tire out too quickly.

IDENTIFYING ROUTES

In the gym, often more than one route shares space on the wall. The differentiation between routes is often marked by tape. If you want to climb a specific route, that route is designated with the same color of tape. When every hand- and foothold is marked with a piece of tape, this is called tracking. Tracking is the most common method of route distinction. A lesser used method of identifying routes uses the same colored holds. This eliminates the use of tape, which easily tears off from scraping climbing shoes. But as the holds become covered in chalk, it is hard to stay on route. Furthermore, the hold selection for route setters is limited when sticking to the same color.

Near the first handhold of a climb is its labeled grade. To climb the described grade, only use the hand- and footholds identified by the route. Using additional holds makes the climb easier, but the idea of marked routes is to use the designated hand- and footholds while climbing. Near the starting hold may be any other instructions for the route, like wall features that are on or off route or any use of feet. For gyms with highly textured surfaces, hand features may or may not be on route, so check with the route setter.

TYING IN

After determining which route to climb, find the appropriate rope to use. This should not be too confusing with a well-laid-out gym. The last hold of the route must be positioned near the top-rope anchors. If not, the potential swing of falling near the finish of the route can be dangerous.

Often, the climber and belayer must choose which end of the rope to tie in to and which end to belay from. As in choosing the correct rope, the climber's end of the rope should travel to the nearest anchor point at the top of the climb. Avoid any tangles or twists around the ropes when setting up.

FIGURE EIGHT FOLLOW-THROUGH

Also known as the figure eight retrace, the figure eight follow-through is the most widely used tie-in knot in gym climbing. The symmetrical pattern of the finished knot makes identification easy.

There are several different methods to tying the figure eight retrace, but the end results are all the same. After tying the initial figure eight, check that the tail end of the rope is about 4 feet. Holding the knot to the harness and having the tail touch the ground is a good indicator of length for most adults. Feed the rope underneath the connection webbing between the leg loops and up through the waist belt where the belay loop connects. Do not position the rope against the body at the waist belt. If only attached to the connector webbing between the leg loops, the climber's center of gravity is lowered in a fall, increasing the risk of inversion. Tying only into the waist belt creates significant force on the climber's lower back in the event of a fall.

When threading the end of the rope through the harness, keep feeding the rope through until the figure eight is mere inches from the harness and maintain that distance while finishing the retrace process. A knot tied far away from the harness leaves a large loop that can catch on holds and pushes the entire knot system far away from the climber. Avoid twisting the strands while retracing the figure eight; keeping the knot loose makes retracing easier. Upon inspection, two parallel strands of rope create the figure eight pattern and a little less than a foot of rope tail is left over for the backup knot.

DRESSING AND SETTING

For knot tying, neatness counts. The finishing touches on any knot are making sure it is neat and tight. Dressing the knot allows the climber to work out unwanted twists or adjust segment lengths of the rope. There is no excuse for a less than perfect knot every time you tie in. Force applied to a loose knot creates a substantial amount of rope movement. Set the knot by tightening it before use. For the figure eight retrace, pull opposite strands of the knot for setting.

BACKUP KNOT

After the figure eight follow-through, securing the excess tail is good practice. Tying half of a double fisherman, also

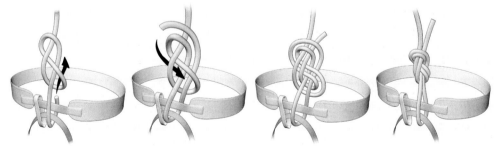

When tying the figure eight follow-through, be sure to leave enough tail after the initial figure eight before retracing the knot. Keep the knot loose until complete, dressing and setting it at the end. (Illustrations by Sam Hanks)

Always tie a half double fisherman backup knot with the leftover rope from the figure eight follow-through. The backup knot should be tight and up against the figure eight. (Illustrations by Sam Hanks)

named the grapevine knot, minimizes the risk of the figure eight untracing itself. The redundancy of this backup knot also keeps the end of the climbing rope out of the way while climbing.

The most common mistake when tying the backup knot is directing the two wraps of the rope away from the climber. Be sure to wrap toward the climber. In addition, one wrap is not secure enough and has a tendency to untie. If there are more than two wraps of rope available, making a few additional wraps is acceptable, but does not provide more security than two.

A correctly tied backup knot has parallel wraps on one side of the knot and crossing strands on the other side. Once finished, the backup knot tightens up against the figure eight retrace. Any space between the knots minimizes the backup knot's effectiveness. After dressing the knot, set it by pulling the end of the rope away from you and pushing the backup knot toward the figure eight retrace with the other hand.

KNOT CHECKLIST
- The rope threads through the connecting webbing of the leg loops and the waist belt.
- The figure eight retrace knot is close to the harness.
- The figure eight pattern of the figure eight retrace is visible and is created with untwisted parallel strands of rope.

■ The half double fisherman has two wraps around the rope and butts up against the figure eight retrace.

Technically, the climber is ready to climb, but must wait for the belayer to ready herself. Additionally, a series of checks and commands must take place to ensure both members of the party are prepared (discussed under Commands, later in this chapter).

BELAYING

The belayer holds a significant amount of responsibility for the safety of the climbing team. While the climber concentrates on upward progress, the belayer's primary responsibilities are to maintain proper rope tension, be prepared to hold and secure the rope if the climber falls, and to respond to the commands of the climber.

Without any climbing-specific gear, holding the rope of a falling climber would be difficult and unsafe. The thin diameter of the rope is too skinny for hands to hold. Even if the belayer were able to keep the rope from slipping, a heavy climber would pull a light belayer off balance or even up in the air. To help create enough friction to securely hold the rope and secure the belayer to the ground, belay devices and anchors are safe belay practices.

GETTING SET UP
Tubular Belay Device
From the belaying strand of the rope (the climber is tied in to the other end), create a

bight, or loop, of rope. Push the bight of rope through the top of the belay device so the bight lines up with the cable of the belay device. If there are variable configurations for the belay device, start by using the one that produces the most amount of friction, referring to the device's instructions.

Attach a locking carabiner through the bight of rope and belay device cable, then clip it directly to the harness's belay loop. Get into the habit of immediately securing a locking carabiner once clipped and then checking the locking mechanism. Assess the lock by trying to squeeze the gate open. Visual checks are unreliable and it is

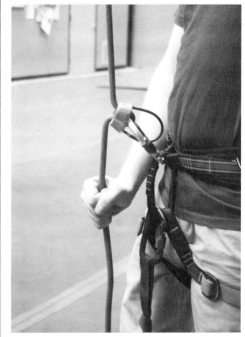

A properly loaded belay device

possible to mistakenly screw the gate open when trying to further close it.

When looking down at the belay device attached to your harness, the rope should travel through the device on the same side as your dominant hand. For smooth lowering, the widest end of the locking carabiner is nearest the belay device. Make sure the rope traveling up to the climber from the belay device is on top of the strand that travels to the ground.

Anchoring

Climbing gyms strategically place floor anchors near the base of climbs. These pieces of nylon cord or webbing are secured to the floor, providing a direct attachment point for the belayer. This prevents belayers who are significantly lighter than their partners from being pulled off the ground. Anchors are advantageous since the belayer remains stationary and they make for easy lowering. New belayers should consistently anchor themselves until they are able to dissipate the force of a falling climber through proper stance and body positioning.

Using an additional locking carabiner (not the one attached to the belay device), connect the floor anchor to the belay loop below the belay device. If there are multiple attachment points on the floor anchor, attach the carabiner at the height of your belay loop. Too much slack in the anchor can pull the belayer off the ground until the anchor is pulled tight. The floor anchor must be short enough to take the force of the climber. Achieve this through a straight line between the floor anchor, belay device, and top-rope anchor.

The belayer's stance affects the force of a falling climber. If the belayer stands back from the anchor, a forceful fall can pull him forward and to an abrupt stop by the floor anchor. Stand forward when anchored to minimize pull from a fall. Keep the anchor to the side of the belayer, not between the legs. The belayer should stand with the legs slightly bent and body angled a bit into the wall to keep the anchor running to the side.

BELAYING WITH A TUBULAR BELAY DEVICE
The Brake Position

As the climber ascends, the belayer must pull slack from the rope through the belay device. When the climber needs to weight the rope, either by choice or from a fall, the belayer manually brakes the rope to keep the climber still. For most climbers, the brake hand is the dominant hand, or the one you would use to throw a ball or write with. The brake hand firmly holds the brake strand directly below the belay device. This position creates a series of bends in the rope at the belay device, producing enough friction to hold the force of a climber. With the brake hand in position, the holding force is in the belay device, so the rest of the body stays relaxed.

At any moment, the belayer must be able to go into the brake position. There are several ways for a belayer to effectively do his task, but they all stem from the golden rule of belaying: *The brake hand must remain on the brake strand at all times!* If the climber were to fall and the belayer's brake hand were not on the brake strand, disaster would likely result. The belay technique described allows the belayer to maintain contact between the brake strand and brake hand at all times.

Taking in Slack

Starting position. Start by holding the brake strand (the end of rope coming from the belay device that does not lead to the top of the climb) about an inch away from the belay device with the brake hand. Position the brake hand so the thumb is closer to the belay device than the pinky. This grip is more ergonomic for braking and lowering. The guide hand (nondominant hand) grasps the climbing strand of the rope extending up to the top-rope anchor.

Alternate brake-hand positioning. Some climbers are uncomfortable gripping the brake strand with the thumb pointed toward the belay device while taking in slack. It is acceptable to change the hand position so the pinky is pointed to the device, as long this is done before belaying begins. Since the brake hand always stays on the brake strand, the belayer must hold her brake hand grip throughout the lowering process, too.

Pull phase. From the starting position, the guide hand pulls rope toward the device as the brake hand pulls rope out of the device. To allow the rope to freely run through the belay device, the brake strand of rope should run parallel to the climbing

An alternate grip for belaying. If using this hand positioning, do not change it before or while lowering the climber.

end of the rope. Pull the brake strand up to chest height and then back down to the brake position. If the brake hand travels higher than eye level and the climber falls, excess slack between the brake hand and belay device increases the climber's fall.

Recovery phase. Repositioning the hands back to the starting position is the goal of the recovery phase. The difficulty lies in keeping the brake hand in contact with the brake strand. For the beginning belayer, completely take the guide hand off

of the climbing strand. Leave the brake hand still, and firmly grasp the brake strand. With the guide hand, reach below the brake hand (next to the pinky), grasping the brake strand. Keeping contact with the rope, slide the brake hand near the belay device. Do not let the brake hand touch the belay device, since a fall at this point will pull a bit of rope through the device and potentially any part of a too-close hand. Let go of the brake strand with the guide hand and return the guide hand to its starting position on the climbing strand. Now the hands are in the starting position and ready to repeat the belay stroke.

If the climber ascends at a constant rate, the belayer constantly takes up slack. Since the belayer may not always see the slack in the system, especially at the climber's waist since the climber blocks the belayer's line of sight, take in slack at the same rate of

movement as the climber's waist. If the climber is not moving, the belayer's hands should wait in the brake position. In the case of an unexpected fall or slip, the belayer is already in the brake position and need not take any extra steps to catch the climber. As noted before, the belayer must be prepared to engage the brake position without warning.

Although learning these belay steps may seem mechanical at first, the ultimate belay flow seamlessly repeats the belay stroke as dictated by the climber. Proper rope tension on the climber is important. If the there is too much slack, the climber may fall excessively, and too much tension on the rope interferes or can even pull the climber off the wall. As belaying becomes more comfortable, learn to belay by feel. When the guide hand is extended and holding on to the climbing strand in the

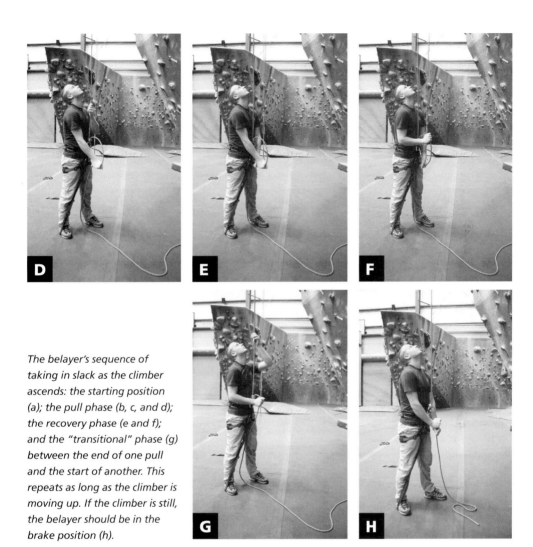

The belayer's sequence of taking in slack as the climber ascends: the starting position (a); the pull phase (b, c, and d); the recovery phase (e and f); and the "transitional" phase (g) between the end of one pull and the start of another. This repeats as long as the climber is moving up. If the climber is still, the belayer should be in the brake position (h).

starting position, gently pull on the strand. This will not interfere with the climber, but when she does move up, the guide hand will drop and then the brake hand can pull rope through the belay device.

Giving Slack

If the climber needs to reverse moves, or downclimb, the belayer will need to feed out rope or give slack. The belay stroke is simply reversed. The brake hand feeds rope into the belay device while the guide hand pulls rope out. Still maintain contact between the brake hand and the brake strand, conservatively feeding out rope in small increments.

Lowering

To lower a climber, the belayer modifies the brake position to decrease the friction, and the weight of the climber pulls the rope through the belay device. The belayer must be in the brake position and the climber weighting the rope. This is usually the case after a fall, but at the top of the climb, the climber must let go of the wall to weight the rope before being lowered. For additional lowering security, place the guide hand above the brake hand in the brake position.

When the climber is ready to be lowered (as communicated by a series of commands described under Commands, later in this chapter), the belayer maintains the brake position but eases the grip on the brake strand. The weight of the climber combined with the decrease in friction slides the rope through the belay device, lowering the climber. The belayer completely controls the climber's descent. Lower in a controlled, consistent manner keeping the hands still. If the hands move up toward the belay device, pinching is probable and compromises the climber's descent. Keep the brake arm straight, easing arm tension and preventing the hand from sliding up to the belay device. If lowering too quickly, the belayer can stop the climber by firmly grasping the brake strand and then can restart the descent at a slower pace.

Lowering a climber should be effortless for the belayer, so keep the shoulders relaxed throughout the process. Guide the climber down until his feet are firmly on the ground and the last commands are used.

BELAYING WITH A GRIGRI

The Petzl GriGri is a widely used belay device in climbing gyms. While heavier and more expensive than a tubular device, its self-braking mechanism backs up the belayer's brake position. Although it can make belaying more comfortable (both physically and mentally), it is not idiot-proof and still requires attentive belaying. Because the lowering action is so different and more sensitive than a tubular device, the GriGri requires practice and instruction before using with a climber. If possible, first learn how to belay with a tubular device: because the GriGri uses a self-locking mechanism instead of requiring the belayer to manually hold the rope in the brake position (as with a tubular device), it is difficult to move from a GriGri to belaying with a tubular device.

Getting Set Up and Belaying

Pay special attention to the instructions that accompany the GriGri. To load the belay device, slide it apart along the rotating pin. With the inside exposed, lay in the belay end of rope. The strand of rope traveling up to the climber leaves the device from the "climber" figure on the GriGri. The brake strand comes out from the "hand" illustration. Close the device and clip a locking carabiner

Even with a GriGri, maintain the brake position when the self-braking mechanism is loaded.

through the open hole in the GriGri, attaching it to the belay loop with the climber's strand nearest the body (with the plastic lever pointing away from the belayer).

As with any belay device, assess the setup with a preclimb check. Tug on the climber's strand of the rope traveling out of the belay device. This pull is similar to the climber weighting the rope, causing the self-locking mechanism to engage.

After using the proper commands to check the readiness of the climbing party

(see Commands, later in this chapter), taking in slack with a GriGri is identical to belaying with any other belay device. However, with stiff, thick-diameter ropes, the belayer may experience more resistance pulling rope through a GriGri. The advantages of a GriGri are evident once the climber weights the rope and the self-locking mechanism engages. The locking mechanism inside the device pushes a lever against the rope. When locked, the brake strand requires little pressure to keep it from slipping, but keeping a secure grip backs up the device. Even with GriGri, keep the brake hand on the brake strand at all times.

Giving Slack

The GriGri works like a seat belt in which the rope can travel through the device in both directions, but when slack is pulled quickly out of the device, the locking mechanism engages. If the climber needs slack from the belayer, giving slow, short pulls prevents the GriGri from locking. If giving slack too quickly and the device locks, stop the pull to disengage the lock, and then restart again.

Lowering

If the climber weights the rope and the belayer tries lowering the climber by easing the grip on the brake strand (like with a tubular device), nothing would happen because the device is locked. It remains locked unless the climber unweights the rope or the belayer uses the device's lowering lever.

Before lowering with a GriGri, position the brake strand of rope so it travels over the curved edge of the device. Keep the brake hand on the brake strand at all times. Lower the climber by gently pulling back the plastic lever with the guide hand.

With the brake hand still holding on to the brake strand, grab the plastic lever on the device with the guide hand and rotate it up until you feel a change of tension against the lever. By pulling back farther than the initial point of tension, the pressure point on the rope opens, allowing rope to slip through the device and lower the climber. Be particularly careful lowering a climber, as the lever is extremely sensitive and there is a fine line between locked and fully open (causing the climber to free-fall to the ground!).

When lowering with a GriGri, focus on controlling the climber's descent by using the guide hand on the lever and with the brake hand backing up the descent from the brake strand. Just like with a tubular device, keep the brake arm straight, preventing the hand from creeping up into the belay device. If the climber descends too fast, let go of the lever to immediately stop the climber, but keep the brake hand secure. This seems counterintuitive, especially after learning how to belay with a tubular device, so although a GriGri may look like an easy device to use, it requires practicing a new set of skills.

PUTTING THE SYSTEM TOGETHER

CONDUCTING A SAFETY CHECK

Redundancy is an important practice in safe climbing. Not only is equipment backed up, but the climber and belayer should practice redundancy in checking each other out for proper gear setup. Distractions are frequent while putting on a harness or tying in to the rope, so each member of the climbing party should check the other for safety. Mistakes like un-doubled-back buckles and unscrewed carabiners happen before the climber even leaves the ground, so double-checking your partner can minimize risks associated with these types of mistakes.

Double-check each other before climbing every time. Since the belayer anchors himself and is immobile, the climber may have to move to the belayer. To keep the checkup systematic, start from the body and then outward toward the rope. When checking your climbing partner, it is a good idea to verbally inform him of what you are checking and its condition.

Checking the Belayer

- **Harness.** The buckles are doubled-back, harness fits securely over the hips at the waist, and the webbing lies flat against the body.
- **Anchored.** If using an anchor, attach it to the belay loop below the belay device. If not using an anchor, consider the consequences of a forceful fall. The belayer's stance should be forward and not straddling the floor anchor.
- **Belay device.** For a tubular device, a locking carabiner clips through both the device's cable and the bight of rope. With a GriGri, compare the brake strand and climber strand with the diagram on the device. Tug test the climbing strand to test the locking mechanism.
- **Carabiners.** Double-check locking carabiners with a squeeze test. Do not rely on a visual check or twist the lock.

Checking the Climber

- **Harness.** No different than checking the belayer: Make sure the buckles are doubled-back, harness fits securely over the hips at the waist, and web-

The climber should double-check the belayer before climbing.

bing lies flat against the body.
- **Rope.** The rope feeds through both the leg loops and waist belt.
- **Knot.** For the figure eight retrace, see that the knot is tied, dressed, and set correctly, and that the backup knot is sufficient. Tie the primary knot and backup within a foot of the climber's harness.

COMMANDS

Many climbing accidents and incidents result from miscommunication between the climber and the belayer. This is from either misunderstanding or the inability to

The belayer should also double-check the climber.

hear a verbal command. If the climber and belayer use the same set of commands, the chance of misunderstanding decreases.

Since the climber takes on greater risk than the belayer throughout the climb, she initiates the commands and the belayer responds verbally or with a directed action. The commands start after the party checks each other and the climber is ready to ascend.

Once the preclimb check is finished, the climber questions "**On belay?**" asking the belayer if he is ready to do his job. The belayer responds by pulling up all the slack in the top-rope system and assuming a solid belay stance. Once ready, the belayer says "**Belay on**." From this point forward, the belayer is ready to

catch the climber's fall at any point.

Once the climber is ready to step onto the wall, the last command before leaving the ground is "**Climbing**," letting the belayer know the climber is about to leave the ground. "**Climb on**" by the belayer is a confirmation that the belayer is aware of and ready for the climber's ascent.

As the climber ascends, she may want the belayer to perform certain tasks. For instance, she might need more or less slack while climbing or might want to weight the rope at some point. If the climber is ascending quickly (or the belayer is taking slack up too slowly), the climber commands "**Up rope**." The belayer then takes up slack more quickly, but not to the point of creating too much tension on the rope between the climber and belayer. If the belayer pulls too much rope in or the climber needs to step down and the rope is constricting movement, stating "**Slack**" prompts the belayer to feed out a bit of rope.

If at any point the climber needs to weight the rope, she commands "**Take**." This tells the belayer to take up the climber's weight and the climber can use this command at any point on the climb. In response to "Take," the belayer immediately assumes the brake position. If the belayer is in the middle of an arm pull taking in rope, he quickly finishes that stroke then brakes the climber. If the belayer has been effectively taking in slack as the climber ascends, the climber will not fall far when leaning back onto the rope. There is no technical verbal response to "Take," but the belayer can say "**Gotcha**."

A similar command to "Take" is "**Falling**." This is often said if the climber is in the action of falling. In response, the belayer immediately brakes the climber.

Once the climber has weighted the rope, eventually she will either climb or be lowered. If she chooses to keep climbing, saying "Climbing" lets the belayer know her intentions. However, if the climber is ready to lower, she can command "**Lower**." The belayer then says "**Lowering**" and lowers the climber.

Last but not least are the commands that finish the working relationship between the climber and belayer. Once the climber is lowered to the ground and no longer needs the assistance of a belay, she says "**Off belay**." The belayer acknowledges with "**Belay's off**" and now can take his brake hand off the brake strand. Indoor climbers often fail to use these final commands because standing on a flat, padded floor makes it fairly obvious when the climber finishes. However, these commands are essential when climbing outside and the situation is not so obvious, so practice the full set of commands to help develop the habit. Be diligent with the exact commands. If your partner yells "Take up the slack" and you only hear "take" and "slack," what do you do? Stick to the commands to limit confusion.

AUTO-BELAY SYSTEMS

In recent years, auto-belay systems have grown in popularity. Auto-belay systems allow for belayer-free top-roping. While some systems operate on pneumatic engineering and others with a flywheel, they work by constantly creating upward tension on a rope or webbing. At the base of the climb, the climber clips into the system with a provided locking carabiner or two. As the climber ascends, the system slightly tugs upward. When the climber weights the rope or webbing, the system automatically lowers the climber to the ground.

The benefit of an auto-belay and the lack of a belayer is that the climber can perform laps on the wall. Disadvantages of auto-belays are the constant upward tension of the device and the fact that once you fall, you are instantly lowered to the ground, eliminating any chance to rest by hanging on the rope and then continuing climbing from the same spot.

Auto-belays are great when you do not have a partner. Take a few practice falls near the ground to get a feel for the descent.

CLIMBING COMMANDS

Climber	Meaning	Belayer's Response	Meaning or Action
On belay?	Ready to belay?	Belay on	Belay ready
Climbing	I am climbing	Climb on	Proceed climbing
Slack	Need rope to work with	(Action)	Feed out rope
Up rope	There is too much slack	(Action)	Take in some more rope
Take	Take my weight	(Action)	Brake position
Falling	I am coming off	(Action)	Brake position
Lower	Lower me	Lowering	Lower the climber
Off belay	I am done with the belay	Belay's off	Verbal acknowledgment

KEY EXERCISE
Learning How to Top-rope Belay

The Challenge

When top-rope belaying, the belayer must quickly react to the climber's actions, comfortably and intuitively taking in slack and assuming the brake position. Smoothly lowering a climber is also a practiced skill.

The Goal

Effortless and natural-feeling belaying with the confidence to brake a climber quickly and to smoothly lower a climber with control.

The Equipment

- Harness
- Belay device and carabiners
- Top-rope system
- Partner
- Floor anchor if available

Before belaying a climber in a "live situation," practice taking in slack and going into the brake position.

The Setup

Grab a top-rope climb for this exercise. A climbing wall is not even needed, since this exercise is a practice in top-rope belaying. You can hang a rope over something high and sturdy if practicing this exercise outside of the gym.

Ground School Top-rope Belay Exercise

1. Load the belay device as if you were going to belay a climber.
2. Have your climbing partner tie in to the other strand of rope (so he can practice tying in). There should be plenty of slack on his side of the rope.
3. Go through the preclimb checklist and commands with your partner.
4. Continuously take in slack, simulating a climber's ascent. Have your partner watch your technique.
5. At various times, your partner simulates a fall by pulling forcibly down on the rope. Go into the brake position to hold the fall.
6. Practice lowering your climber with him hanging on the rope.

Considerations

Treat this exercise as if you were actually belaying. The only difference is that your partner is on the ground.

You must be extremely proficient at this exercise before belaying a live climber.

This exercise is still effective in practicing the belay motions without a partner and is not limited to a climbing gym.

This exercise can also be practiced with a GriGri, but do so only after developing competent use of a tubular belay device.

CHAPTER 4

Movement Technique

For most people starting out with climbing, the main objective is to get to the top of the wall or route. While the satisfaction of this accomplishment may be an incentive to keep climbing, most people strive to challenge themselves by climbing more difficult climbs as their ability improves. One way to climb more difficult routes is to become physically stronger, but these improvements are limiting. Climbing is often perceived as an upper body–intensive activity, in which the number of pull-ups you can do is an indicator of how hard you can climb. Just after a few climbs though, it would be evident to anyone that climbing technique and movement skills play a more important role in climbing movement than raw strength. The fastest and most efficient way to become a better climber is by improving your technique.

This chapter focuses on learning the proper climbing technique on vertical to less-than-vertical terrain. Many of these principles are true for overhung climbing and roofs, but there are differences in the actual climbing techniques. Chapter 6, Bouldering, focuses on the techniques specific to steep terrain. However, it is important to have a solid foundation of the skills discussed in this chapter to be a proficient all-around climber.

TYPES OF MOVEMENT

Climbers characterized as smooth and graceful are often displaying static movement as opposed to dynamic movement. Static moves are stable movements initiated and maintained via musculature. For example, standing on the tips of your toes to reach a hold rather than jumping to it is static movement.

The primary advantage of static

movement is control. Static climbing requires balance throughout the move. This balance allows you to let go of a handhold or foothold and reach or step to the desired position. Your body is stable while you reach, so you have the opportunity to search for the best part of the handhold or be ready to shift your weight back onto your foot. If you can pause in the middle of the move, you are climbing with static technique.

Static movement is what every beginning climber should strive for since it forces proper body positioning and balance. However, static movement has its limitations. If you simply cannot reach the hold from a static position, dynamic movement is a more appropriate technique for extending reach.

Dynamic movement is momentum-based. The body is set in motion in an attempt to "carry" itself to a hold. The most extreme form of dynamic movement would be flight, when a climber jumps up to latch onto a hold. However, more subtle forms of dynamic movement would be small jabs to holds that the climber cannot reach in a static position. A disadvantage to dynamic movement is that once the body is set in motion, there are no last-second opportunities to correct body positioning. In addition, you have only one chance to grab the best part of the hold you are shooting for and stick to it. (See Dynamic Movement toward the end of this chapter for an elaboration of this technique.)

PERFECT PRACTICE

There is the saying that "practice makes perfect." This is only true to a point, since whatever you practice is what you perfect, and practicing bad habits is not helpful in the long run. Consider instead that "perfect practice makes perfect." It is just as easy to ingrain bad habits as it is to learn good habits. If you "just climbed," you might get better, but inefficient habits will become so learned that your progress will be limited. Deliberately practicing the foundations of climbing movement will speed up learning and allow future progress with ease.

CHARACTERISTICS OF A GOOD CLIMBER

The next time you are in the gym, look around at the people climbing. Try to point out someone who you think is a good climber, regardless of how hard or easy their climb is. Perhaps you have already noticed some good climbers. Consider what about that person makes them a good climber.

Good climbers have the ability to shift from one move to another without interrupting their movement. This is called flow and without it, climbing movement looks jerky, interrupted, and maybe even desperate. To achieve this flow of movement, the climber looks as though he already knows what every move is supposed to be like and which holds to use and when. Each move is deliberate with little wasted movement. While performing moves, a good climber will make them look effortless and will seemingly float up the wall. An often made analogy is that great climbers look

as though they are dancing up the wall. As a dancer's movement is dictated by the rhythm and sound of the music, a climber's body positioning is dictated by the holds and features on the wall.

In line with this analogy, there are many steps in climbing—just as in dancing—that must be mastered before advancing in complexity. For example, before you can dance, you must learn some basic steps and footwork. Before that, a strong command of walking is necessary. And on the most basic level, you must be able to stand and have basic balance skills. Climbing movement must be approached the same way. A sound sense of balance, proper weight shifting, and foot precision are key components that lead to total body movement.

WEIGHT SHIFTING

The general principle for all types of climbing is getting as much of your body weight on your legs as possible and pushing off them for upward movement while using your upper body to help maintain balance and posture. Because of this, your ability to shift your weight over your feet is a fundamental skill. This is true for all types of climbing terrain, although there are some modifications in body positioning on steep, overhanging climbs.

The ability to control your center of gravity is called weight shifting. Generally, a woman's center of gravity is in the area of the hips, while a man's center of gravity tends to be a bit higher. If you were to stand with your feet shoulder-width apart with weight evenly distributed on both feet, your center of gravity would pull down directly between your feet, splitting your body in two.

Looking back at the dancing analogy, you must learn to walk before you can dance. From standing with your feet shoulder-width apart, consider what your center of gravity must do to allow you to step forward. To step with the left foot, your center of gravity must shift over the right foot to free up the left. The same weight shifting occurs in climbing, but the difference is stepping up, not forward.

The width of your stance plays a significant role in weight shifting. When your feet are close together, your center of gravity only needs to move mere inches to shift your weight. Wide stances require your center of gravity to move much farther. Another benefit of a close stance is maximum reach, but consider that standing with your feet close together is not very stable. The best of both worlds, for getting started, is standing with your feet shoulder-width apart.

When you shift your center of gravity, it is important that the movement comes from your hips, not your upper body or shoulders. Leaning is not sufficient for complete weight shifting. Proper weight shifting comes from deep bends in the legs, allowing the hips to move back and forth. Horizontal weight shifting should occur before moving up.

Pay attention to how close your center of gravity is from the wall. On vertical terrain, the closer you are, the more weight your legs are sustaining and your arms will be less taxed. In actuality, your center of gravity will move slightly away from the wall while you are stepping with your feet, so it is essential to pull your hips close into the wall between moves. Visualize a string attached to your belly button, pulling yourself tight into the wall. Your shoulders should be arched back a bit, allowing you to look up and around at your environment. Avoid hugging the wall with you upper body, for this creates the tendency for your hips to sag away from the wall.

Although we can make parallels between walking and stepping up while climbing, the use of hands in rock climbing tends to complicate weight shifting. When walking on the ground, you have no other choice than to effectively shift your weight to step forward. However, since climbing is perceived as an upper body–intensive activity, climbers tend to overuse their arms, simply because they can. What often happens is that a climber grips holds with her hands, and instead of properly shifting her weight from one foot to the other, body weight is supported by her arms instead. This even happens with advanced climbers with underdeveloped footwork and weight shifting. Overuse of your upper body will cause you to tire quickly.

A sequence of weight shifting using only the hands for balance. Take note of how the climber's center of gravity shifts before moving, stepping, or standing. For stepping up or out, the center of gravity must be moved over the supporting foot to free up the moving foot.

Because you can stand on your feet all day long but only hang from your arms for a few minutes, minimize pulling with your arms as much as possible.

FOOT PRECISION IN WEIGHT SHIFTING

Pay attention to using the inside edge of your foot when standing on holds. Edging is the most common type of foot placement. Using the inside edge allows you to rotate your foot around the hold for better balance, keeps you in line with your center of gravity when shifting your weight, and allows you to stand on your toes to gain maximum height. When using the inside edge of your foot, it is important to create contact between the hold

Using the inside edge of the foot. The heel is raised to give the climber maximum height and put more pressure on the toes.

KEY EXERCISE
Learning proper weight shifting
The Challenge

Climbing is often perceived as an upper body–intensive activity, but smooth and efficient movement comes from properly shifting your center of gravity over your feet. By learning how to move by pushing with the legs and using only the hands for balance, you are less likely to overuse your upper body and you will tire less quickly.

The Goal

Balanced, controlled, smooth movement on less than vertical terrain initiated from the legs.

The Equipment

- Less than vertical climbing wall
- Climbing shoes
- Several large footholds big enough to stand on with both feet

The Setup

Position the footholds near the ground creating a horizontal traverse. They should be relatively close together and the height of each hold should vary no more than one foot from the next.

No-hands Traverse Exercise

1. Using the palms of your hand against the wall for balance, step onto the leftmost foothold from the ground with your right foot.

KEY EXERCISE
Learning to climb with the legs
The Challenge

The importance of efficient footwork and body positioning while climbing cannot be emphasized enough. Climbers have a tendency to "pull down" on holds, even when it is not necessary.

The Goal

Upward climbing movement generated more by pushing with the legs than by pulling with the arms. This exercise is very similar to the No-hands Traverse Exercise but is geared toward vertical rather than horizontal movement.

The Equipment

- Harness
- Climbing shoes
- Top-rope setup
- Belayer
- Very easy route

The Setup

Tie in to the rope as the climber. The climb should be very easy with a lot of footholds and handholds. Do not worry about staying on an established route.

2. Once balanced on your right foot, bring your left foot next to it on the hold.
3. Shift your weight from your right foot onto your left foot. This should free up the right foot so you can move it.
4. Step to the next hold with the right foot. Shift your hips over your right foot to take weight off of the left foot.
5. Repeat these steps until the end of the traverse has been reached then come back in the other direction.

Considerations

Slightly use handholds for balance if necessary.

Remember to fully weight and un-weight your feet before moving. Laterally shift, and then stand.

Move slowly enough that you could stop your movement at any time. Avoid falling onto holds and practice stepping down as much as stepping up.

Pay attention to your Balance Checklist (page 74).

The angle steepness of the wall, size of the footholds, and the spacing of the holds all contribute to the difficulty of this exercise. Changing any one of these can make the exercise more or less difficult to suit your current level of balance and movement. Once you feel comfortable performing the exercise, increase the challenge.

Low-hands Climbing Exercise

1. Climb a route keeping your hands as low as possible. Shoot for not reaching above your head.
2. Since climbing with low hands limits your ability to pull down on holds, reach out to the sides and use handholds to help you shift your weight from side to side and gain vertical ground by pushing with your legs.

Considerations

Start this exercise on a less-than-vertical wall and then work up to more challenging terrain. Remember, the idea behind these exercises is not just to get to the top of the climb, but to learn though the exercise itself.

As you feel more comfortable with this exercise, try to position your hands lower.

Since your hands are only used for lateral pulling in this exercise, they should not be tired at the end of the climb.

Climbing with low hands is not recommended as a regular climbing style, but as an exercise it is effective in forcing deep weight shifting.

and the outside edge of your toe. This allows for your foot to rotate on that single point to adjust body positioning. In this balanced and frontal position, your toes will be pointed out in a duck-toed fashion. This is helpful when stepping since it allows the hips to stay close to the wall. If you stepped up with your feet pointed straight into the wall, your hips would be pushed out, creating more weight for your arms to bear.

BALANCE CHECKLIST FOR VERTICAL TERRAIN

- Keep as much weight on the inside edges of your feet as possible with your heels up for maximum reach.
- Maintain an upright posture to limit slouching.
- Pull your hips toward the wall, like a string pulling your belly button over your feet.
- Relax your upper body.

FOOTWORK

As previously mentioned, edging is an often used form of foot positioning. However, there will be many instances where there is no edging platform on which to stand. Consider the following alternatives.

KEY EXERCISE
Learning to stay in balance while maintaining an even distribution of weight
The Challenge
Overgripping with the hands, unbalanced movement, and excessive stabilization from the upper body are all factors that contribute to jerky moves and tiresome climbing. Overcome these burdens by paying attention to the amount of grip force exerted, to whether or not you feel balanced, and to how much weight your arms are bearing.
The Goal
Using light hands while climbing, keeping movement balanced and stable, and maintaining an even distribution of body weight.
The Equipment
- Harness
- Climbing shoes
- Top-rope setup
- Belayer
- Easy-to-moderate climb
The Setup
Find a route that you have comfortably climbed without falling. Be sure to go through the proper checks and commands with your belayer before climbing.

Stepping in a pocket.

POCKETS

For pocketlike holds in an indoor environment, there are usually two options when using them as footholds. If the pocket is big enough or your shoes are amply pointed, place as much of your toe box in the hold as possible and use the front edge of the toe box. If that does not provide enough security, try standing on top of the entire hold. The ability to use pockets as footholds is somewhat dependent on your footwear. Rental and beginner's shoes usually have a very rounded toe that is less than desirable on small to moderate pockets.

Hand/Foot Pause Exercise

1. With every hand move, hover your hand a few inches from the hold for a count of three before grabbing it. In that pause time, ask yourself:

    Is my weight distributed over my feet?

    Can I relax the grip I have on the other hold?

2. Take your time to be sure that you pause for every handhold.

3. After you have completed the climb, repeat the exercise. This time, hover your foot above each foothold instead of pausing your hand. During the pause, ask yourself:

    Can I put more weight on my standing foot?

    Can I position my body to take more weight off of my arms?

Considerations

Do not get on climbs that are so difficult that you cannot pause.

Only pause your hands *or* your feet. Combining the two of them into one exercise can be overwhelming and can produce robotic climbing.

SMEARING

Sloping edges are more difficult to stand on, since the foot has a tendency to slide off of the hold. The more surface area between the hold and your shoe, the better the friction. Smearing is the most exaggerated form of standing on a sloping hold, used when there simply are no footholds to step on. This technique relies solely on creating enough tension and surface area between the sole of the foot and the wall. Dropping the heel below the toes and leaning the body away from the wall pushes the climber's center of gravity in toward the wall instead of down to the ground. This method does create a lot of stress on the arms because of the limited amount of weight that smearing can hold before the foot slips.

HEEL AND TOE HOOKS

Rather than stepping on a hold with the edge of your foot, hooking the hold with your foot can sometimes be a more effective way for your feet to support your body. Heel hooks are often used on overhanging faces, while pulling roofs or around corners (also known as arêtes). The advantage of placing your heel on or around a foothold is that it provides a solid platform from which to pull your hips closer to the hold. In this instance, it would be more difficult, if not impossible, to get your toes around the hold and pull in. Do not be afraid to pull in tight with your hamstrings to get your

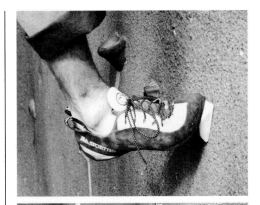

Smearing. The heel is kept low to increase surface area between the sole and the wall. Because of the insecure nature of smearing, the arms are kept straight and the hips and thus the center of gravity are kept away from the wall to drive the climber's weight into the wall at the feet.

A heel hook around a corner

Toe-hooking allows the climber to use the top of the foot to pull the body closer to the wall.

hips locked in close to the wall. The higher you can position your hips, the closer the next handholds will be.

Toe hooks are used in similar instances to heel hooks, but the toes are flexed up toward the knee and locked into that position. From this locked position, your foot can be used as a hook, latching onto underclings, corners, and the back side of holds. To stay locked into position and to keep your hips from sagging, pull your foot toward your hips to maintain body tension throughout the move. Solid heel and toe hooks are a sneaky way to find rests on every type of terrain.

TOE AND FOOT JAMS

Jamming your hands or feet into cracks is usually reserved for outdoor rock climbing, but these techniques should not be overlooked by the indoor climber. Some gyms have beautifully sculpted crack systems and there are holds designed as cracks. You can even use crack techniques on two holds placed close together or in a corner.

If you are stepping into a crack with your right foot, roll your ankle to the outside, so the sole of your foot is facing to the left. In this position, you toes are perpendicular to the ground and your knee points out to the right. Slide your toes into the crack as far as they will go. To secure the jam, rotate your knee so it points straight up. This will provide the torque needed to keep your foot secure and now it can be weighted. If you relax the pressure created on your foot in the crack at any

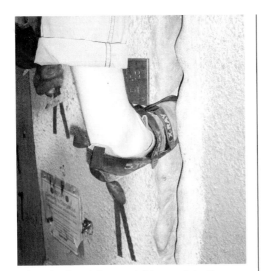

After the foot is inserted sideways into the crack, the knee rotates upward, locking the foot into place.

point during the movement, your foot will likely slide out.

FLAGGING

We do not always have the luxury of two solid footholds to stand on or move from. Often, there is only one foothold that allows for efficient body positioning. In these instances, adjust your center of gravity using your upper body for positioning so that as much of your weight is on that one foothold as possible. This may require you to rotate your body to use the outside edge of your foot. The foot without a hold can then "flag" against the wall with its inside edge, helping to stabilize the body. This flagging foot acts

Flagging with the inside edge. With the handhold and foothold vertically lined up, most of the climber's weight is on the standing foot, and the flagging foot acts as a balancing rudder.

like a rudder by pushing against the wall, keeping the hips close to the wall and over the weighted foot. If the holdless foot is not placed against the wall and left to

An outside-edge flag, pinning the hips close to the wall

dangle, it can create a barn door effect. That is, the holdless foot swings away from the wall and pulls the rest of the body with it.

Flagging with the outside edge of the foot can be helpful, too. In this position, the weighted foot is using its inside edge. The flagging foot can either be crossed through your body between the weighted leg and the wall, or it can be positioned behind the weighted leg, pinning it against the wall. Most often, outside-edge flagging is most effective when the latter technique is employed.

STEMMING

Stemming is an effective way to rest inside of corners, or dihedrals. By pushing with your feet against the walls of the corner, a substantial amount of weight can be taken off your arms. Your hands can also stem by pushing away from each other. This can free up a foot to step up and make vertical progress.

HIGH STEPS

When stepping up on footholds positioned near the waist, flexibility can be a limiting factor for some people. Even if you can get your foot on the hold, using it to your full advantage can be difficult. For high foot placements, focus on pointing your knee out to the side of your body when stepping up. If you step up with your knee pointed into the wall, your hips will be pushed back from the wall, causing you to fall away from the wall. Once your foot is on the hold, shifting all your weight onto your foot can be difficult, since you are performing a one-legged squat to push your body up the wall.

KEY EXERCISE
Learning foot placement and precision

The Challenge

When advanced climbers perform their art, their movement speaks for itself. With less advanced climbers, the thud of a misplaced foot against the wall says a lot, too. Noise from a climber's foot scraping or sliding down the wall to reach a foothold results from sloppy foot placements. This comes either from imbalanced movement or not paying enough attention to the desired target.

In ball sports like soccer, baseball, or golf, if the participant takes his eyes off the ball too early by looking in the anticipated direction of travel, contact with the ball is less likely. The same holds true for climbing. A common mistake is looking down to find a foothold only long enough for the foot to get near or above the hold. At the last second, there is a tendency to look up for the next move. This premature search for holds produces a margin of error in foot placement.

The Goal

The purpose of this Key Exercise is to prevent the common "touch and slide" placement, that is, putting the foot against the wall and grinding it down until it lands on the hold. This grinding makes the climber unable to put the foot in the maximum weighted position on the hold because the foot interferes with the climber's line of vision. The excessive grinding also quickly destroys the climbing shoe's rubber. "Quiet" feet force the climber to move more slowly as well, due to the desire for efficient placement.

The Equipment

- Harness
- Climbing shoes
- Top-rope setup
- Climbing route
- Belayer

The Setup

Pick a route that you are interested in climbing. It can also be a traverse. Your belayer or spotter (if on a traverse near the ground) can help you by pointing out your loud footwork.

Quiet Feet and Stare-down Exercise

1. Climb a route with an emphasis on keeping your feet as quiet as possible.
2. For every hold that you step on, make sure that you focus on the hold and "stare it down" until your foot is firmly placed on the hold.
3. Your belayer or climbing partner (if you are traversing near the ground) should announce every time she hears your footwork.

Considerations

Not only is this an exercise, but it is also what you should strive for in your climbing on a regular basis. Precise footwork will give you confidence and you will not have to second-guess your foot placements.

BODY POSITIONING

Where a handhold is located dictates how you grab the hold and what body positioning is required to allow you to hold onto it with as little effort as possible. Since your arm can rotate in front of you 360 degrees, there are endless possibilities of where a hold is in relation to your body. Consider the following four positions and the body positions they require.

STRAIGHT ON

This is the most basic and natural hand position. Reaching up and grabbing the top of the hold is a straight-on position. The palm is facing away from the climber, toward the wall, and the fingertips are above the wrist. Keep your arm as straight as possible. This allows the bone structure in your arms to take your body weight. A bent arm flexes the muscles and can speed up fatigue.

UNDERCLING

The opposite of grabbing a hold straight on is an undercling. With this type of grip, the hand is rotated inward so the palm is facing away from the wall. The closer the hold is to the body, the easier it is to

The classic straight-arm rest position. If the arms are bent, more muscle activity is required to hang from the hold.

With an undercling, position the hips close to the undercling so the hold can be "pulled down" near the waist, using the biceps and pulling the hips tight against the wall.

maintain control. Grabbing an undercling at full arm extension requires significant body tension, so the closer the hold is "pulled down" to the hips, the more stable the body becomes, because the biceps are used to pull the hips in. The sooner you can get your feet up and bring the hold closer to your body, the better. Although they can be found on all types of terrain, look for underclings in roofs.

SIDEPULL

Reaching out on a face to grab a corner is a classic example of using a sidepull. With

The climber is leaning away from the sidepull to create body tension, allowing the reach with the left hand.

this grip, there is no way to pull down on the hold, so you must shift your weight to lean away from the positive side of the hold, creating enough tension for stability or movement.

GASTON

The gaston is a sort of "pushing" sidepull. If the positive part of a sidepull is facing you, use a backhanded grip to reach for the hold with your palm facing outward. To create tension on the hold, shift your weight toward it as much as possible. Keep you elbow pointing away from your body if possible and maintain pressure with your foot on the opposite side of the handhold. This position can create a lot of stress on the shoulders, so practice it with care.

HAND GRIPS

In addition to using your hands in body positioning, various holds require different grips.

EDGES

Ranging from pencil thin to large enough to sit on, edges make up a significant portion of the grips we use in climbing. The size and angle of the edge determine how to grab the hold. The easiest types of edges are incut, which allow the fingers to slide to the back of the hold and stay relatively secure there. Sloping edges are difficult to grab since there is no "positive" grip on the hold, and the fingers are

A gaston move. The climber is most comfortable with the center of gravity near the gaston hold. As the climber reaches out left, a rigid line of tension is created between the right hand and the left foot, increasing the pressure felt on the shoulder. Be cautious and listen to your body while doing moves like this.

fighting just to stay in contact with the hold. Consider the following types of grips on edges.

Crimping

Crimping is holding onto an edge with the second knuckle pointing up. The thumb can be added for additional force and stability. This grip is very strenuous, since your body weight is placed on the joints of your fingers. The pads of your fingertips are in contact with the hold surface and are bent back at the first joint. Because crimping requires less hand strength than an open hand grip, beginning climbers tend to use this grip more often. Finger injuries usually involve crimping.

Crimp positions in which the pads of the fingertips are on an edge and the knuckles buckled up put a lot of pressure on the tendons and ligaments of the hands. Putting the thumb down over the fingertips (left) can secure the crimp, but intensifies force on the ligaments.

Open Hand

An alternative to crimping is the open grip. This position is more tendon friendly since the knuckles are not buckled back so severely, but it requires more forearm strength because the tendons and forearm muscles, rather than the joints, absorb body weight. Try to grab edges in an open grip as much as possible to help prevent finger injuries. You may find it difficult at first, but the strength will come quickly.

POCKETS

Pockets can range from handlebar-like jugs to sloping one-finger nightmares. Like

A three-finger pocket grabbed with an open hand grip

stuffing your feet into climbing shoes, pockets generally require the same idea. By stacking your fingers in a pocket, the pressure that is created increases the friction and creates a more secure hold. The more fingers you can get into the hold and the deeper you can sink them, the better.

PINCHING

Grabbing a hold with an open grip and using the thumb to squeeze the hold is pinching. Anything from as wide as a telephone pole to as thin as a cigar-sized hold can be pinched, but the difficulty lies in creating enough force in the hands and forearms to grasp the hold. The wider the grip, the more difficult it is to create force on the hold.

An open hand grip on the same hold as the crimp grip. The hand is in a more open, anatomic position, allowing the forearm muscles to help stabilize the forces on the hand. This is preferable to crimping, but requires more hand strength.

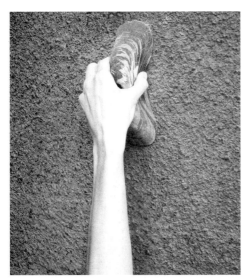

Squeezing (pinching) a hold with fingers and thumb can require a lot of force. The larger the hold, the more difficult it is to grab.

SLOPERS

Sloping holds are the trickiest set of holds to master. Since they slope down away from the wall, the surface area is such that your hands feel like they are slipping and sliding right off the hold. Because there is no incut area to dig your fingers into, the keys to hanging on slopers are surface area and direction of pull. The more of your hand that is in contact with the hold, the more friction created and the better you will grasp the hold. On large slopers, consider contacting the hold not with just your hands, but with your wrists and forearms, too. Also, keeping your center of gravity low and beneath the hold will prevent you from sliding off the hold.

Slopers require the most subtle technique. Maximize the surface area between the hold and the hands by keeping the elbows close to the wall. When getting set up to move off of a sloper, keep the center of gravity low. This is particularly important when reaching with the free hand. If the center of gravity raises too much, the elbow of the arm that is hanging onto the sloper will rise, causing the hand to slide out.

When pulling the hold down and raising your body to move past the sloper, maintain that downward force by keeping your elbow directly under the sloper. Raising the elbow will change the direction of pull from down to out, spitting your hand off the hold.

HAND JAMS AND FINGERLOCKS

Although not common in climbing gyms, holds that require hand jams and finger-locks are an important part of a climber's repertoire of grips. Hand jams work by vertically placing your hand into a crack and then increasing the thickness of your hand to the extent that the pressure created against the inside of the crack is enough to keep your hand secure. Look for a constriction in the crack and place your hand in right above it, so the crack narrows right below your hand. From this position, slide your thumb down the palm of your hand. This increases the thickness of your hand, causing it to stay securely in the crack. Pressure must be maintained or your hands will slip out of the crack. Hand jams can be done with the thumb facing either up or down.

Fingerlocks are similar to hand jams. When the crack is so narrow that you cannot slide your hand into it, just your fingers can be used. The fingertips are placed into the crack as far as they will go, then the palm is twisted down, thus locking the fingers into place.

Hand jams and fingerlocks are not the most comfortable types of hand positions,

Using fingerlocks with the upper hand and a solid hand jam with the lower, this climber looks solid in this sculpted crack.

especially without taping your hands, but they do have their time and place for successful climbing.

SWITCHING HANDS AND FEET

You may find yourself in a position where you want to switch your hands or match both hands on a particular hold. If the hold is large enough, taking one hand off and replacing it with the other is not very difficult. Although with small holds, you should take a few fingers off of the hold at a time and replace with fingers of the free hand. It also helps to make room for the match by providing space on the hold for the new hand. The difficulty of matching is not with the hands, since you can replace one finger at a time, but with matching feet.

When matching your feet on large holds, simply make enough room to place both feet on the hold. If you cannot get both feet on the hold, try rolling one foot off the hold and rolling the other foot onto the hold in the same smooth motion. This technique is not as effective on tiny footholds and nubbins.

The hop-step method of exchanging feet is most commonly used on smaller footholds. With this method, place the free foot directly over the weighted foot. It should hover mere centimeters over the supporting foot. In one smooth motion, pull the weighted foot out and step down with the free foot onto the hold. It takes a significant amount of practice to switch out your feet without scraping the wall with the stepping foot and to achieve a precise landing. When performed quickly

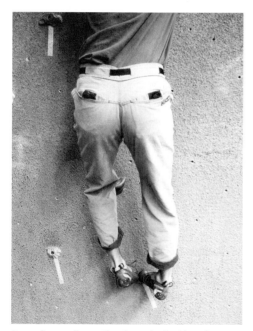

For a foot roll match, place the inside edges close enough together to roll one foot off the hold and the other onto it at the same time.

The hop-step is a quick way to switch the feet on a hold. Although the free foot is touching the top of the standing foot, it is not applying any pressure.

and efficiently, the upper body should have to take up very little additional weight.

The disadvantage of the hop-step is that you can never see the hold you are stepping on. You can only feel with the weighted foot and make a good estimate of what the hold is like. For microfootholds, this may be inadequate and more precision may be needed. Switching your feet out by smearing is a more precise method than foot hopping. If you are standing on a hold with your left foot, smear your right foot against the wall near the hold, freeing up your left foot. Then, smear your left foot against the wall near the foothold. With both feet smearing for just a moment, you can then see the foothold and use pinpoint precision when placing your right foot on it. Because both feet are smearing for a moment, this technique puts more strain on the arms than the hop-step, but it allows for more precision.

A foot exchange using the smearing method. Although this requires more moves than the hop-step, it is a very precise method for tiny holds.

KEY EXERCISE
Learning how to interchange hands and feet on holds
The Challenge
There are often occasions when you want to replace one hand with the other on a hold or one foot with the other. Sometimes this results from being out of sequence, or maybe the route requires switching out your hands or feet.

The Goal
Quick and smooth transitions when switching one hand or foot for the other.

The Equipment
- Climbing shoes
- Different-sized footholds
- Different-sized handholds

The Setup
Position the handholds at about chest height and the footholds near the ground. Make sure the footholds provide a stable enough base for a comfortable stance. The holds should range from big enough for matching hands or feet to micro sized. Vary the style of holds, using everything from slopers to pockets to edges.

Switch Out Exercise
Hands
1. Start with a comfortable stance on the footholds, with one hand on a handhold.
2. Practice taking one hand off of the hold while putting the other one on. Take your time when taking your fingers off and try to make room for the new hand.
3. As you feel more comfortable and the movement becomes smoother, move on to progressively smaller holds.

Feet
1. Stand with one foot on the largest foothold. Grab holds with your hands that allow the most comfortable body position.
2. Replace your standing foot with your free foot using the following methods:
   - Foot roll
   - Hop-step
   - Smearing
3. Move on to progressively smaller holds as your technique improves.

Considerations
Be creative with hand positions to make room for switching out your hands. Consider pinching different parts of the hold or stacking one hand on top of the other.

A lot of time and energy can be wasted trying to switch out your feet. For the hop-step, position your free foot as close to your weighted foot as possible before switching feet. Keep your arms straight while smearing.

Practice the foot switches until you feel confident and smooth on even the smallest of holds.

KEY EXERCISE
Learning to climb by feel
The Challenge

Of all of our senses, sight often takes over as the primary receptor. Because of this, the decisions we make while climbing are mainly sight dependent. But much of the visual stimulation we take in is irrelevant to climbing, and we can become overwhelmed with information. Making judgments based on sight, we may shy away from holds that look sloping or too small to use. Also, the more dependent we are on sight, the less importance spatial awareness is. The ability to know how your body relates to the environment is invaluable, saving time wasted visually searching for footholds that have already been used as handholds.

Climbing blind can help overcome this challenge. Not only does blindfolded climbing help develop spatial awareness and feel, but it also forces your body to climb statically and to stay in balance. When you search with your hand to find a hold, the rest of your body must be in balance to compensate for the time that the free hand is searching. This is true for the feet as well. Note that dynamic movement is only effective when seeking predetermined targets and ineffective while climbing blind.

The Goal

Develop special awareness, the sensation of climbing by feel, and climbing "in the moment" without visual distraction.

The Equipment

- Blindfold
- Top-rope setup
- Harness
- Belayer
- Climbing shoes
- Very easy, less-than-vertical route

CROSSING THROUGH

Once you have developed a keen sense of balance and footwork in the frontal position, it is time to focus on moving smoothly and efficiently. However, we rarely climb in a straight line like ascending a ladder. Even when you are climbing straight up, you often make subtle lateral movements. So far, our attention to weight shifting has been on side-to-side movements, but that is not always the best course of action.

In walking, these lateral movements are made by shuffling and then matching your feet. This is fine for traversing, but if you were walking up to an obstacle and had to get around it, you would cross one foot over the other to change your direction of travel. That same principle holds true for changing lateral direction in climbing. From traversing to moving a few feet to the side, crossing through with your hands and feet is often more efficient than shuffling them. By crossing your hands and feet over each other, you can

The Setup

Make sure that there are enough holds on the climb. Remember, you will be blind-folded so staying on route is impossible. Tie in to the rope and check your belayer before putting on the blindfold. Make sure your belayer lets you know when you are near the top.

Blindfolded Climbing Exercise

1. Take your time stepping onto the route. To stay in balance and find holds, you will be climbing much slower than you would normally.
2. When searching for holds, make large sweeping motions and search in all directions.
3. The belayer should be silent during this exercise. Giving verbal guidance will only distract the climber from the task at hand. The belayer should announce to the climber when he is near the top.
4. Take off the blindfold before being lowered to the ground.

Considerations

This is also a great exercise for climbers who are anxious about climbing or height. It enables them to focus solely on climbing and not on the discomfort of being off the ground. They must be prepared to take their blindfold off at the top of the climb, though.

This exercise is most effective on easy, less-than-vertical terrain. Increase the challenge by limiting the number of holds, rather than increasing the steepness of the terrain.

do half as many moves more fluidly.

If you are traveling to the left, rotate your body to face that direction. Rotate your right shoulder toward the wall and cross through your body to the left. Use the grasp of your right hand to help shift your weight over your left foot. Once your right foot is free, cross it through your body and place that foot to the left of your left foot. Follow that by releasing your left hand and reaching out to the next hold. After stepping out with your left foot again, you will be in your starting position.

Crossing through is never as easy as 1, 2, 3, but the idea is for hand and foot movements to complement each other. If you traverse too far with just your arms, your feet will be left behind and you will find yourself off balance and ready to barn-door off the wall. Lead too far with your feet and you will be in a tangled mess trying to get your upper body to follow. At times you may have to match or interchange your hands or feet to stay in balance as you cross through.

Cross-through sequence. Notice how the hands and feet move together, helping the climber stay upright and balanced.

DYNAMIC MOVEMENT

All the movement thus far described in this chapter pertains to static movement. Since static movement is more controlled than dynamic movement, it is often the preferred method of movement. However, static movement is limited to holds that are

KEY EXERCISE
Learning how to laterally move by crossing through

The Challenge

Rarely does a climber move straight up. There is often some lateral movement in ascending. Although such movement may range from subtle moves to horizontal traverses, there are smoother and more effective ways to move sideways than by shuffling the hands and feet. Crossing the hands and feet between the climber's body and the wall is most effective.

The Goal

Developing lateral movement skills that combine efficiency and smoothness.

The Equipment

- Climbing shoes
- Footholds
- Handholds

The Setup

Set up the holds in a horizontal traverse with a variety of grips. Put up more than are needed to allow for a variety of movements.

Cross-through Exercise

1. Start by getting on the traverse to the right side.
2. Cross your right hand through your body, reaching to the left. Your right hip should be angled toward the wall and your upper body should be facing to the left.
3. Keep moving left by stepping through with your right foot.
4. Before stepping with your left foot in the same direction, be sure to shift your weight over your right foot.
5. Continue a combination of hand and foot cross throughs until you reach the end of the traverse, and then head back to the start.

Considerations

It may not be feasible to cross through with both your hands and feet for every move. Shuffling, matching, or switching out your hands or feet may be necessary at times to stay in balance.

Try to stay upright throughout the exercise. Leading too far with your hands or feet will cause an imbalance in body positioning.

As the traverse becomes smoother, limit the number of holds you use.

A further challenge is completing the entire traverse with as few foot- and handholds as possible.

within your reach, which are determined by your strength, body positioning, and balance. Momentum-based dynamic moves are often the only choice in extending your reach or making an off-balance move. They can be performed as subtle deadpoints to holds a few inches away or as all points off the wall dynos several feet away.

DEADPOINTS

Imagine that you are on a vertical wall, standing on decent footholds. Your right hand is on a decent hold and your left is on a poorly sloping hold that you cannot hold onto very well. You do not have the strength or body positioning to allow you to take control of the left-hand sloper and reach up with your right hand. In this case, a momentum-based deadpoint is the solution.

If a ball were thrown up into the air, it would eventually slow down to the point where it would momentarily stop in midair, and then travel back down to the earth. The apex of its flight is the deadpoint, or the point at which there is no movement. To apply that to our climbing scenario, you want to move your body toward the hold with enough momentum so that when you reach your deadpoint, the hold is close enough to grab. Because your momentum is carrying you toward the desired hold, your left hand does not require full control of the bad sloper.

The key to all dynamic movement is initiating movement from the hips. If you can get your center of gravity traveling, the distance the hold is from your reaching hand lessens, making reaches easier. The common mistake climbers make with dynamic moves is reaching with their arms instead of with their hips. Reaching with the hands too early in a dynamic move causes the hips to move away from the wall to counterbalance the reach.

In a perfect deadpoint, the hips are pushed toward the desired hold. This is done with the legs, and the arms provide secondary support in the movement. As soon as the hips have reached their apex, the reaching hand moves toward the hold, continuing the momentum of the movement. As soon as you grab the desired hold, be prepared to stabilize your body. The momentum you have created must eventually be controlled.

KEY EXERCISE
Learning to dynamically move from bad holds
The Challenge
We are not always strong enough or in the right body position to securely grab onto holds and maintain control. At these times, momentum-based dynamic movement is the preferred technique in making further progress.
The Goal
To move dynamically off of a poorly gripped hold to the next. *—continued on next page*

—continued from previous page

The Equipment
- Climbing shoes
- Several handholds
- Several footholds

The Setup
Position several footholds near the ground. The handholds should be placed so that there are both positive and difficult to grab handholds on both sides of your body. At your midline, place a decent handhold within reach above your head.

Good Hold/Bad Hold Exercise
1. Step onto the footholds in a comfortable stance and grab a good hold with your right hand and a poor hold with your left.
2. The idea is to move your right hand on the good hold up to the other hold above your head. Your left hand will remain on the bad hold during the movement.
3. Before you move your right hand, center your gravity over your feet.
4. Once centered, use your legs to push your hips up and toward the targeted hold.
5. As your hips start to slow from the upward momentum you have created, quickly move your right hand to the hold.
6. Be prepared to control your momentum as soon as you latch onto the desired hold.
7. Switch which hand you use for the good hold/bad hold setup.

Considerations
Depending on the amount of balance you can maintain from weighting your feet, and the distance to the targeted hold, the momentum from your hips can range from a subtle shift in your hips (by pushing slightly with your legs) to more dramatic movement initiated from your legs and requiring you to pull with the good hold.

For the good hold/bad hold exercise, the climber's left hand is on a poor open-hand pinch. Using momentum generated from the center of gravity, the left hand only needs to stay still while the right hand latches another good hold.

DYNOS

Dynos are exaggerated deadpoints. The most extreme dynos require the climber to completely leave contact with the wall, travel though the air, and latch onto another hold. The same principles of deadpoint movement still apply.

To set up for a dyno, get your feet high and underneath you if possible. The higher your feet, the more you can push off them and the closer they are to the desired target. Often, a pumping action with the hands and feet are helpful to develop some initial momentum and position the hips over the feet. Once you are ready to fly, explode by pushing with your feet when your hips are over them. There is a tendency to push the body away from the wall, so use your hands to pull yourself in toward the wall.

Just like deadpoints, delay reaching with your hands for the target until your momentum is starting to slow down. Reach too early and you may lose all your momentum. Reaching with one hand to the target allows the other hand to stay on the starting hold for longer, but latching on with one hand can be difficult after such a long move. If the target hold is big enough, consider a double-handed approach. The commitment level is higher, but it's much easier to regain control with two hands than one.

For long dynos, the climber starts with his feet as close to underneath him as possible. The explosive movement comes from pulling the body in toward the wall while the legs push up.

PUTTING ON YOUR DYNAMIC GAME F.A.C.E.

Focus

Focus your attention on the task at hand. If you are a static climber or are not comfortable with dynamic moves, psychologically adjust to a shift in your movement.

Aim

Take a good look at your target. Decide which hand to reach with and what part of the hold to grab. As you travel toward the hold, your perspective of the target will change, so visually eye in on it and keep it locked in your sights.

Commit

Commitment comes before you do the move. Release yourself from reservations and give yourself the confidence you need to follow though.

Execute

You cannot just sit there all day planning the move. Now is the time to know that you have taken a logical approach to the move and it's time to fly.

KEY EXERCISE

Learning to dyno far distances

The Challenge

Sometimes holds are simply out of static reach. However, with a lot of commitment and some momentum, bridging long gaps of several feet between holds is possible.

The Goal

To perform dynos with one and two hands through momentum-based movement.

The Equipment

- Climbing shoes
- Several large handholds
- A few footholds
- A vertical to slightly overhanging wall
- A padded floor and/or bouldering pad
- Climbing partner for spotting

The Setup

Position a hold large enough for both hands at about chest height. Set up a vertical line of a few large handholds starting a bit higher than head height. Set up the footholds in a few horizontal lines below the starting handhold, giving multiple options for height.

—continued on next pages

—continued from previous page

The Two-Handed Dyno Exercise

Although starting with two-handed dynos may be more difficult than one-handed dynos, it is a more effective way to reinforce dyno technique.

1. Grab the starting hold with both hands and sink your hips low so your arms are straight. Your hips should be square with the wall and your toes set so there is at least a 90-degree bend in your knees.
2. To initiate the dyno, drive your hips up the wall toward the target by pushing with your legs. Your arms should pull your body in toward the wall.

Letting go of the starting hold for two-handed dynos requires a lot of commitment. Let go and reach for the target holds when the torso and hips are at their peak height.

—continued from previous pages

3. When your hips start to slow down, reach with both hands to the targeted hold.
4. As you feel more comfortable, target the progressively higher holds on the wall.

The One-handed Dyno Exercise

This is not much different than the above exercise. In this case, only one hand is reaching for the targeted hold.

1. Grab the starting hold with both hands and sink your hips low until your arms are straight.
2. Decide which hand you are going to reach with. You may want to angle your hips so that the side of your body that you are reaching with is toward the wall. This twisting position can give you some extra extension.
3. To initiate the dyno, drive your hips up the wall toward the target by pushing with your legs. Your arms should pull your body in toward the wall.
4. If your hips are angled at all, the driving upward force will come from the leg that is closest to the wall.
5. Because the hand that remains on the starting hold is stable as the other hand reaches through the air, it is difficult to let go with that hand at the end of the move. Thinking of pushing off that stable hand at the end of the move will help you let go.
6. As you feel more comfortable, target the progressively higher holds on the wall.

Considerations

Performing this exercise as a top-rope is not recommended. It is difficult for a belayer to take up slack when the climber is performing long dynos and there is the possibility of getting the rope wrapped around the hand midflight.

A competent spotter is needed for this exercise in order to minimize the risk of the climber falling back if the targeted hold is missed. Spotting is discussed in detail in Chapter 6, Bouldering.

Momentum must be maintained through the lower body driving the hips up. Extension can be made all the way down through the toes.

Do not forget to put on your dyno F.A.C.E.!

SEQUENCING

Even through sequencing is more a mental aspect of climbing than a physical technique, it is the most significant factor in smoothly stringing individual moves together. Sequencing is the ability to look at a route and determine what moves to do and how to do them. This involves everything from finding the starting holds to determining what direction the climb travels. If you aimlessly grab holds, you are less likely to find yourself climbing the route's path of least resistance.

Sequencing improves your climbing by enabling you to do fewer moves and to achieve better body positioning, and by enhancing your ability to anticipate difficult or confusing sections of the route and to identify easy sections for rests. The four main approaches to sequencing are from the ground up (preclimb), while climbing, after falling, and after climbing.

PRECLIMB

The preclimb sequence is also known as ground-up sequencing, which takes place before you actually climb the route. At this time, try to gather as much information as possible about the route. Identify the general direction of the climb, find all the holds, and locate any natural features like corners. Also, identify difficult sections that you may have a hard time with, but look for easier sections where you can rest. Take note of any technical potential hazards like big top-rope swings or tricky lead-climbing clips.

WHILE CLIMBING

Once you have gathered the big picture and are climbing, in-climb sequencing allows you to anticipate moves up to four or five holds in front of you. If you focus on too much of the route, like the anchors, it is easy to miss holds in your immediate reach. Conversely, too much attention paid to the holds within your grasp can lead you astray. If your pre- and in-climb sequencing skills and climbing technique come together well enough, then you will find yourself at the anchors, having successfully completed your climb.

AFTER FALLING AND AFTER CLIMBING

Yes, at some time you will fall on a route. Instead of pouting, take this opportunity to figure out if there are any technical options to the sequence you just fell off of. Since you're already hanging on the rope, take a minute before jumping back on the route. Look around—perhaps there are holds you did not see or use.

Get back on a few moves lower than when you fell and in the same seqence. From here, figure out a new way, if need be. The idea is not to just get through the moves, but to figure them out for future success. As soon as you get off the route, go through the sequence postclimb. This helps burn the sequence into your memory. In actuality, figuring out the sequence postclimb is simply preparing for the next preclimb sequencing on the same route.

CHAPTER 5

Lead Climbing

Although top-rope climbing has many advantages—it is the easiest introduction to roped climbing, skill requirements are basic, falls are generally short and gentle, and you do not have to worry about dealing with your safety system as you climb—it also has limitations. For example, top-roping extremely overhung or wandering routes can be unsafe, since falling off can result in big swings that can endanger you or others in your path. Another limiting factor is that many climbing gyms dedicate only a portion of their total wall surface to top-rope climbing. Knowing only the skills necessary for top-roping also limits your route choices if you should choose to start climbing outdoors, as only those areas where routes can be accessed from above to set anchors will be available to you.

These constraints can be overcome by broadening your skill set to include lead climbing—a mode of climbing in which, rather than climbing on a rope already anchored at the top of the climb, you take the rope up as you climb and affix it to progressively higher anchor points along the way. In a gym environment, these anchor points generally consist of a quickdraw (two carabiners attached to one another by a piece of nylon webbing, also known as a draw) attached to a fixed bolt. Outdoor leaders protect their climbs by placing protective gear in the rock or by clipping draws to fixed bolts.

Lead climbing allows for a freedom that top-rope climbing cannot provide. Once you are a proficient leader, your choice of gym routes will be limited only by your skill. You will also be able to explore terrain not previously available to you, such as meandering routes or those that go through large overhangs. Because lead climbing involves setting anchor points in addition to moving up the wall, it is more mentally engaging than top-rope climbing.

Lead climbing has its own constraints and considerations, however. For example, instead of worrying about big top-rope swings, you must be prepared for longer falls than in top-roping—a leader who falls from a point above the last clipped bolt travels the distance to that bolt and then that distance again. Consequently, falls are significantly different from those experienced in top-roping, as they involve longer airtime that ends with a sudden jerk as the rope pulls taut. Leading also requires greater endurance, poise, and efficiency than top-roping the same grade, since you must stop several times during a lead route to pull up slack with one hand and clip the rope into the quickdraw.

HOW THE LEAD SYSTEM WORKS

Both lead climbing and lead belaying require even greater focus and care than top-rope climbing and belaying. Decisions must be made quickly as the belayer reacts to the climber and vice versa. Many climbers enter the world of leading through learning to be a competent lead belayer and, in fact, this an excellent way to familiarize yourself with the rhythm, flow, and technique involved in leading. Conversely, learning to lead climb will make you a better lead belayer, as you will develop a keener understanding of the need for efficiency throughout the whole operation. Although you will most likely lead belay before you ever lead climb, begin with the mechanics of lead climbing first, as it is the "action" in the action-reaction system of lead belaying.

LEAD-CLIMBING GEAR

For liability reasons and to monitor the number of lead climbers at a given time, climbing gyms usually provide lead ropes.

Gym lead ropes are thicker, more durable, and shorter than personal climbing ropes. To verify lead-climbing and belaying competency, you must check out a rope from the staff. However, some gyms leave ropes available on the floor. Check with your gym for their policy.

Fixed carabiners attached to bolts are the industry standard for protection. Using steel carabiners or chain links instead of webbing makes these quickdraws more durable. The gates of these draws are heavier than a standard aluminum gate, but work just the same. For the climber's safety, do not grab the carabiner as a hold for clipping, even in desperation or to make a clip. Nylon webbing is difficult to hold and grabbing the carabiner does not allow any room to attach the rope.

LEAD-CLIMBING SKILLS AND TECHNIQUES

RESPONSIBILITIES OF A LEAD CLIMBER: ARE YOU READY?

Because the commitment level of lead climbing is greater than top-roping, it is not something beginners should jump right into. Those attempting to learn how to lead climb should feel confident climbing at least 5.9 on a top-rope. While this is not a magic grade, gyms seldom set lead routes easier than 5.8. And even more important than the ability to hike up a certain grade is a solid foundation in movement and kinesthetic awareness. If your climbing is not yet smooth and graceful, consider putting in more time on your technique before embarking on lead climbing. Remember, as a lead climber, you not only contend with the actual act of climbing, but also with managing and clipping the rope to ensure your safety.

In leading, decisions you make can affect not only your safety but also that of your belayer. To stack the odds of safety in your favor, practice all of the skills necessary to promote safe climbing. Even before mock leading (i.e., leading while on top-rope), carefully review and practice all of the following exercises and skills.

SELECTING YOUR ROUTE AND PREPPING YOUR GEAR

Before tying in to the sharp end of the rope (the lead climber's end of the rope) to begin leading, consider your route and its surrounding environment. Having a real assessment of your own personal climbing will prevent you from getting on routes over your head. If your climbing limit is 5.9 on less-than-vertical routes with decent holds, you should think twice about getting on a long, steep 5.9 covered with crimps.

Also consider the safety of the surrounding environment before getting on a climb. Check to see if other leaders may cross your route or vice versa. If so, wait until they are finished or climb another route. Keep an eye out for miscellaneous gear left at the base of a route and move it if there is any chance of it getting in your team's way. Think about wearing a helmet while lead climbing. The added safety provided by a helmet will give you an increased sense of security, which is comforting, especially for the beginning leader.

TYING IN AND CHECKING OUT

To tie in to the rope, grab the rope end that sits on top of the stack and affix it to your harness using either a figure eight follow-through knot or a double (sport) bowline. Some climbers prefer tying in with the bowline because it is easier to untie after the stress of a lead fall, however, if you are not comfortable with tying this knot, a figure eight will work fine (see Tying In in Chapter 3 for a description of the figure eight).

The sport bowline, also known as the double bowline, differs from a regular bowline by creating two loops of rope to feed the free end though. Do not use a single bowline to tie in. The sport bowline is more difficult to visually check than the figure eight retrace, so take care in tying it correctly and seek confirmation from gym staff. Always back up the sport bowline with half of a double fisherman's knot.

With your belayer, go through the same safety check as you would if you were climbing on a top-roped system, to make sure that the system is "closed," with both of you having properly set up your equipment. Remember, an easy way to perform a thorough check of the system is to start your check with those elements that are closest to your body (e.g., your harness and knot) and then follow the rope through the system, ending with the harness of your belayer. Along the way, you will verify that your belayer has set up the belay device

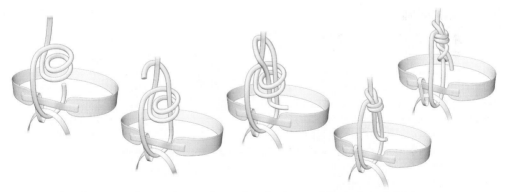

The sport bowline. Note the two loops of rope that the free end feeds though. Make sure your climbing partner learns the sport bowline in order to check it when tying in. One of the reasons leaders like this knot is because it is easy to untie, so always back it up with half of a double fisherman's knot, as shown in the sequence's last illustration. (Illustrations by Sam Hanks)

REFRESHER: CONDUCTING A SAFETY CHECK

Checking the Belayer
(checked by both members of the team)

- **Harness** is on properly with buckles doubled-back or otherwise secured as dictated by style of the harness.
- **Anchored** properly (if anchored belayer is desired or required).
- **Belay device** is properly loaded.
- **Carabiners** are locked.
- **Rope** is properly flaked on the floor and is free of kinks.

Checking the Climber
(checked by both members of the team)

- **Harness** is on properly with buckles doubled-back or otherwise secured as dictated by style of the harness.
- **Rope** passes through necessary points on harness and **knot** is tied correctly.

Just like in top-roping, double-check each other before lead climbing and belaying.

properly and that the rope has been stacked to avoid tangling.

COMMUNICATION

An open line of communication is imperative between the climber and belayer, especially indoors with multiple climbing parties in close proximity. The commands for lead climbing are similar to top-rope climbing. In lead climbing, the commands "On belay" and "Belay on" signify that the belayer is ready, but it should be noted that the leader is not truly protected by the belayer until the first draw is clipped. The command chain presented in Chapter 3, Top-rope Climbing follows from there, but some leaders use, "Clipping!" to let the belayer know that slack is needed to clip the next bolt. If your belayer can see you and is paying attention, however, this call should not be necessary.

REFRESHER: CLIMBING COMMANDS

Climber	Meaning	Belayer's Response	Meaning or Action
On belay?	Ready to belay?	Belay on	Belay ready
Climbing	I am climbing	Climb on	Proceed climbing
Clipping	I am pulling up rope to clip	(Action)	Feed out rope to clip
Slack	Need rope to work with	(Action)	Feed out rope
Take	Take my weight	(Action)	Brake position
Falling	I am coming off	(Action)	Brake position
Lower	Lower me	Lowering	Lower the climber
Off belay	I am done with the belay	Belay's off	Verbal acknowledgment

BEFORE THE FIRST CLIP

Once safety and commands have been established, the climber can start up the wall. Keep in mind, though, that a fall before making the first clip will result in a ground fall. Consequently, there are a couple of precautions you and your belayer may want to take to deal with this.

If the opening moves of the climb are difficult, preclipping the first bolt is not a bad idea. Some lead-climbing purists say this tactic is cheating, but staying safe should be your first priority. If possible, climb up an easier neighboring route, properly clip the rope in to the first quickdraw, and climb back down to the ground. Make sure the role of the belayer is confirmed before you attempt this maneuver because you may choose to downclimb or be lowered from the first bolt.

Another option for protecting a fall prior to the first bolt is having the belayer

Since the lead climber is not protected from a ground fall by the rope until the first draw is clipped, the belayer can spot the climber with both hands until the first clip is made. The belayer must then quickly take in slack and be ready to belay.

spot the climber during the opening moves of the route. With this approach, your belayer will need to first pay out enough slack for you to clip the first draw and will then assume a spotting position as in bouldering (for more details on proper spotting technique, refer to Chapter 6, Bouldering). As soon as you have clipped the first bolt, the belayer takes in the appropriate amount of slack and you will be on belay.

CLIPPING THE ROPE CORRECTLY

The correct way to clip a rope into a carabiner is with the climbing end (attached to the climber) running up along the wall and then out through the carabiner to the climber. An incorrectly clipped, or backclipped, rope passes through the carabiner from the climbing

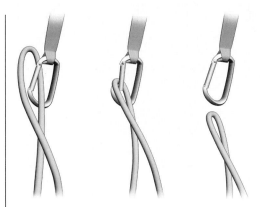

The reality of the rope unclipping from a back-clipped draw (Illustrations by Sam Hanks)

side and then into the wall. Because a backclipped rope can become unclipped in the event of a fall, great care should be taken to ensure that you clip the rope correctly every single time.

Clipping the Rope to the Quickdraw

The mechanics of clipping the rope into a quickdraw (i.e., carabiner and webbing combined) is as simple as it seems; however, applying those mechanics with pumped-out forearms and shaking legs can make things much more complicated. Consequently, the use of practiced, fluid, efficient technique is an absolute necessity.

The following section introduces methods for efficient clipping. Although these are not the only ways you might get the rope into the carabiner, they are among the most commonly used. If these styles

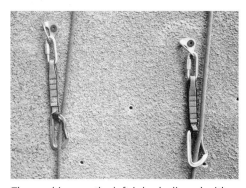

The carabiner on the left is back-clipped with the potential to become unclipped in a lead fall. After clipping the rope into a draw, make sure the rope travels through it as pictured on the right.

do not work well for you, experiment with other approaches. Ultimately, the best way is the one that is the fastest and most comfortable for you. When encountering a quickdraw, the gate will either face toward or away from you. Its positioning determines how you grab and handle the rope before clipping.

Middle finger grab technique. Use this method when clipping a carabiner whose gate is facing the opposite direction of your clipping hand (e.g., gate is facing to your left and you are clipping with your right hand). Stabilizing the quickdraw with the middle finger makes clipping easy. If the carabiner is positioned against the wall on less-than-vertical or vertical terrain, the middle finger can pull the draw away from the wall for trouble-free clipping.

Pinch technique. This technique is used when the carabiner gate is facing in

Middle finger grab technique. Reach down with your clipping hand and grab the rope as if you are shaking hands with it. Pull up the rope and, with your palm facing the floor, place your middle finger through the carabiner and pull down lightly to stabilize it. Your index finger and thumb will pinch the rope. Rotate your hand toward the gate using the middle finger as a pivot to push the rope through the gate with your thumb.

Pinch technique. Pick the rope up as if you are shaking hands with it, but grasp the rope so it is between the tips of your pointer finger and middle finger, similar to holding a cigar. With the palm down and angled toward the draw, stabilize the carabiner by grabbing it in a wide pinch, with your thumb against the spine and your pointer and middle fingers against the gate. Close the pinch, bringing your fingers toward your thumb to push the rope through the gate. Be sure to pass your fingers with the rope all the way through the gate. Trying to pull your fingers back at the last second will cause you to get pinched by the gate.

the same direction as your clipping hand (e.g., the gate is facing to the right and you are clipping with your right hand). Most people find this way of clipping more challenging than stabilizing the draw with the middle finger. Practicing both techniques on a carabiner hanging close to the ground will help you to improve rapidly.

UNCLIPPING

If you clip the wrong quickdraw or backclip a carabiner, unclipping the rope is probably more difficult than clipping it. Regardless which side the carabiner gate faces, grab the entire carabiner and push the gate open with a free finger or thumb. With the gate open, turn the carabiner upside down, allowing gravity to slide the rope out. Let go of the carabiner and make the correct clip. Undoubtedly, the rope will catch on the key-lock groove of the open carabiner, so some creative wiggling helps slide the rope free.

THE DREADED Z-CLIP

One of the benefits of indoor leading is that the bolts are often spaced closer together than you would find on an outdoor route. This limits the length of falls and provides an added sense of security. One drawback, though, is the tendency to Z-clip.

A Z-clip is formed when a lead climber grabs the rope from below an already clipped quickdraw. This results in the rope traveling from the belayer to the highest clipped draw, back down to the lower draw, and then back up to the climber. When this happens, the rope drag is so great that the climber is prevented from moving up. Z-clipping also effectively removes the higher bolt from the system, leaving the lower bolt as the highest anchor point. This creates the potential for longer falls, which are always less desirable.

To avoid Z-clipping, grab the rope directly below the tie-in point at the harness, not farther down the rope. This ensures that when reaching up to clip, the end of the rope is attached to you and is not the middle section below the last draw. If a Z-clip does occur, simply unclip the higher carabiner and then properly reclip.

The climber is about to Z-clip. As he travels up, the excessive drag of the rope running from the climber, down to the lower draw, back up to the higher draw, and back down to the belayer, will keep him from moving up. Avoid this by grabbing rope to clip directly below the tie-in point at the harness.

KEY EXERCISE

Learning how to efficiently clip and unclip quickdraws

The Challenge

While leading, the climber must be able to quickly and safely clip the climbing rope into fixed quickdraws. The more time spent with the rope pulled out to clip, the more potential there is for falling. Often, strenuous body positioning, rope drag, or an awkwardly placed draw adds difficulty to the task. Unclipping is equally important. Backclipping or clipping the wrong draw requires unclipping to correct the problem. This skill is essential when following a lead climb.

The Goal

A quick, efficient clip and unclip performed with either hand, to a draw with the gate facing either left or right.

The Equipment

- Harness
- Climbing shoes
- Quickdraw
- Climbing holds
- Lead-climbing rope

The Setup

Position the quickdraw at eye level on the climbing wall. There should be enough hand- and footholds for the climber to stay on the wall and vary body positioning.

Clipping and Unclipping Exercise

1. Tie in to the rope as if you were lead climbing. Closely flake the rope near the wall.
2. Comfortably position yourself on the wall, just off the ground and within reach of the draw. Although the holds and terrain will dictate your exact body positioning, focus on keeping weight over your feet and relaxing as much as possible.
3. Clip the rope into the carabiner, focusing on efficiency and quickness.
4. Unclip the rope from the carabiner and repeat the exercise until you can quickly and comfortably clip and unclip with either hand and with either gate orientation.

BODY POSITIONING

Because clipping requires the climber to momentarily let go with one hand, body positioning should allow for the most stable and restful stance. It should be similar to a rest stance in which the skeletal system and legs take the weight of the climber, and the body is relaxed. Feet should be still and secure and the quickdraw should be within reach.

The optimal body position for clipping a draw is with the carabiner at chest or stomach height. If you choose to clip from higher above the carabiner than this, you may find yourself forgetting to clip or moving too far past the bolt. If the carabiner is too high above you, you will be forced to take out an excess amount of

Considerations

To practice multiple scenarios, turn the carabiner gate in both directions to use both styles of clipping.

Use creative clipping stances. Roofs can require clipping behind your head, and crossing your arm through the body to clip is not unusual. The more variations practiced, the better prepared you are on a climb.

Practicing clips from different types of holds will foster confidence. Underclings require different body positioning than slopers.

Because the rope is not running though any draws before clipping there will not be any rope drag. To prepare for potential rope drag in the exercise, use the "bite" technique when clipping draws above the chest. By reaching for the second pull of rope while biting the first pull in your teeth, the rope drag will be less on an actual climb.

Confident and quick clips are best learned and practiced on or near the ground.

rope to clip which not only requires more effort but also creates potential for a longer fall.

Imagine, for a moment, that you are clipping a draw that is a foot above your waist and your waist is 10 feet above your last clipped bolt. In this case, 11 feet of rope would be needed to clip your bolt. Now imagine that you are clipping that same bolt from a lower stance so that the bolt is about 4 feet above your waist (i.e., you are reaching over your head to clip). To clip the bolt, you would need to pull enough slack into the system to give you the 11 feet of rope required to span the distance between the two bolts plus the additional 4 feet required for the rope to come back down from the bolt to your waist. In the first case, if you fell while clipping, you would take a slightly longer than 22-foot fall. In the second case, your fall would be a little more than 30 feet. Which would you prefer?

Another thing to consider is that rope drag and friction between the rope and the previously clipped carabiner alters clipping. If several draws are already clipped, or the route changes directions or angles, the drag can be heavy enough to make hauling up enough rope in one pull very difficult. In this case, pull up enough rope to reach your mouth and gently hold it in your teeth. Quickly grab another pull of rope and immediately release the bit between your teeth. *Take care with this practice, as you can imagine the repercussions of falling while biting down on the climbing rope.*

If you are uncertain that the quickdraw is close enough to clip, reach out and attempt to touch it. Try not to contact the carabiner too hard though, because a swinging draw is hard to clip. Once you are ready to clip, make the commitment to clip and follow through the action. As mentioned earlier, you might want to inform your belayer of your intent by saying, "Clipping!" As you pull rope out to clip, keep your entire body still as you execute the move. Any excess movement can throw you off balance or cause an unexpected slip. Keep your eye on the draw until the rope is secured and the gate closed. Rush the process and you may bobble the clip, and have to try again.

THE GROUND FALL ZONE

Just because you have clipped the first bolt does not necessarily mean you are safe from a ground fall, even with an attentive belayer. In fact, the most potentially dangerous area for a leader is between clipping the first and second draws. A fall in this "ground fall zone" can be injurious to both the climber and belayer.

By way of demonstration, assume a quickdraw is established every 10 feet on a route. When you are positioned to clip the second bolt, your waist might be about 2 feet below the draw, 8 feet above the first draw, or 18 feet above the ground. If you were to fall at that point, you would travel a minimum of 16 feet toward the ground (twice the distance from the last draw clipped). Slack in the rope, stretch in the system, and pulling up the belayer even a little would result in a ground fall. A ground fall would be even more likely if the fall occurred while you were pulling rope up to clip the second bolt.

Many gyms try to design their lead routes so that the first and second bolts are close to each other. However, since you are responsible for your own safety, keep in mind the real risks and dangers in the ground fall zone.

ROPE MANAGEMENT

When lead climbing, the rope either travels above you to your highest bolt as in a top-rope system or, at those times when you are above your last bolt, hangs from your waist and dangles about your feet. Without proper rope management, however, what

If this climber falls, he will likely flip upside down because the backstep positions the rope down the back of his leg.

This climber is in the same position as the climber with the backstepping stance (in the previous picture), but here the climber shows better rope management by having the rope run between his legs. This would allow his legs to freely fall away from the wall without catching on the rope.

should be an uneventful fall can become a catastrophic accident.

As a rule, you want to keep the rope between your body (including your legs) and the wall. It is also acceptable to keep the rope between your legs or off to one side or the other. Where exactly you want the rope to run will depend on the line the rope follows below you. Ultimately, what you want to avoid at all times is having the rope pass behind one or both of your legs, and then down to your highest anchor point. This hazard, known as backstepping the rope, puts the climber

in potential danger for an inverted fall.

If the climber backsteps the rope during a fall, as the rope pulls tight the legs become hung up on the rope. The upper body continues to fall, however, causing a headfirst fall. This is extremely dangerous because the back and head will most likely be the first parts of the body to impact the wall. To avoid backstepping the rope, pay close attention to the line your rope takes below you and take great care to dance around it in whatever way is necessary to prevent it from dragging behind your legs.

FALLING

A difficult move, spinning holds, or an unexpected slip can send a climber airborne. Knowing how to take a lead fall is a part of lead climbing. Although falls are often over before you know it, occasionally there is still enough time in-flight to prepare for impact.

As soon as you feel that you are falling, you should gently push out with hands and feet to ensure that your body clears the wall. This is particularly important on vertical or less than vertical terrain. Falling close in to the wall can result in your face or knees scraping the climbing surface. Note that when using this technique, you do not want to push off too hard, as pushing off with too much force slams you into the wall as the rope tightens at the end of the fall.

While falling, keep your hands free from grabbing the rope or draws. You can injure (or even lose) fingers by holding onto a fixed-draw carabiner while falling. Rope-burned hands can result from holding onto the rope as it pulls taut under the impact force.

At impact, feet and hands should be shoulder-width apart with the knees slightly bent. This may require bringing your feet up to cushion your body and absorb the impact and prevent your knees from hitting the wall. Leaning forward during the fall can cause your torso and

arms to slam into the wall before your feet, so be careful. Keep your eyes open and try to watch the wall as you are falling. When the rope is pulled tight and you swing into the wall, look for a spot that your feet can hit that is clear of holds. Falling with a stiff body is the sure way to sustain an impact injury. The fear of falling stems from the fear of the unknown. Taking short practice falls helps alleviate the anxiety of falling.

LEAD ANCHORS

The last pieces of fixed protection on an indoor lead route should consist of two equalized anchors to provide redundancy,

When falling, keep the body loose and relaxed. Rigid positioning will only intensify the impact against the wall. (Illustration by Sam Hanks)

an integral characteristic of any climbing anchor. Depending on the climbing facility, the anchors may be two draws with the gates facing in opposite directions. In this case, clip the rope into both carabiners so that the gates are in opposition. Another popular option is a spring-loaded anchor, a hooked piece of metal with a spring-loaded gate similar to a carabiner gate at the top. With these anchors, lay the rope on the gates from the top and the rope will snap into place. To prevent excessive rope wear, clip the rope into the anchors in the same direction as the climb finishes. For example, if the route finishes by moving

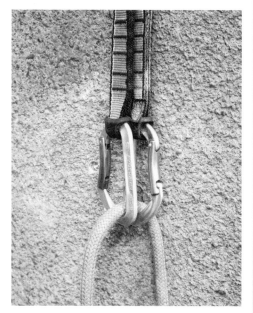

Carabiner anchors clipped opposite and opposed. This is the best configuration for clipping two carabiner anchors.

from left to right, lay the rope in the shut so the climber is lowered on the right side.

LEAD BELAYING

Belaying a leader is much more involved than belaying a top-roped climber. The lead belayer must constantly adapt to meet the movements and needs of the climber—providing slack as the climber is clipping or moving above her last anchor point and taking rope in as the climber moves toward a clipped bolt. Absolute focus from the belayer as well as an open line of communication is imperative for ensuring safety.

ANCHORING THE BELAYER

Whether to use an anchor while belaying a lead climber is an ongoing debate. Although there are pros and cons to anchoring, ultimately, the belayer must decide which method works best for him. Belayers should be comfortable belaying both anchored or unanchored, as some climbing gyms do have preferences so strong as to require the use of only one method.

Choosing to Floor Anchor

Lead falls generate a significant amount of force on the belayer. An attentive belayer can brake any fall, but absorbing the force of the fall can be problematic. When a lead climber falls, the force you experience may be enough to even lift you off of your feet, especially if you weigh significantly less than your climber or if there is a substantial amount of slack in the system. If pulled off your feet, you will likely swing into the wall, potentially compromising your ability to maintain the brake position. In extreme cases, the belayer can even be pulled up to and stopped by the first bolt. The more vertical travel the belayer experiences, the longer the fall for the climber.

Proper anchoring will allow you to remain stationary upon feeling the impact of the climber's fall. Although this impairs your ability to soften the fall of the climber by reducing the dynamic nature of the belay system, stretch and slight slippage of the rope, tightening of the knot, and the little bit that you are pulled even though you are anchored will still absorb some of the force of a fall.

Climbing gyms most often make floor anchors out of webbing or static line that is attached to permanent fixtures in the floor. Usually these anchors will have various clip-in points along their length. Clip in to the point that provides for a tight anchor, but not so tight that your harness is pulled uncomfortably toward the floor. Clip the floor anchor to your belay loop using a carabiner separate from the carabiner that will be clipped to your belay device. Be sure to clip the anchor carabiner to your belay loop at a point below the belay carabiner.

Once anchored, orient your body so that your chest is facing in the direction of the first bolt. Rather than standing with your feet side-by-side, place one leg (the side opposite to your belay hand) farther forward, and slightly bend both knees. This position will help you to plant your weight into your hind leg to resist being yanked forward by even the short distance the anchor may allow.

Ultimately, with proper body positioning and stance, the belay system (with you in the middle) will form a straight line from the anchor point on the ground up to the first bolt. If not already formed, the force of a fall by your climber will create this line for you, snapping you into place in a violent pull.

After your climber has reached the ground and you have taken her off belay, do not assume all potential for accidents has passed. As entertaining as it may sound, you can wipe out pretty good by trying to walk away while still anchored, so do not forget to unclip!

Choosing Not to Floor Anchor

Some argue that there are more advantages to belaying unanchored than to belaying anchored. Without a floor anchor, you have the freedom to find the safest belay stance as the climber moves. For example, you may position yourself to the right of the climber and against the wall until the first bolt is clipped but then may want to move to the other side of the climber at a later time. In the event that slack must be taken in quickly, you can take it up simply by stepping back from the wall. Also, the "give" of an unanchored belayer at the point of impact adds to the dynamic nature of the belay.

If you are new to lead belaying, you may choose to anchor to have the added comfort of knowing you are grounded. However, if you weigh about the same as your climber, the benefits of belaying anchored are diminished, particularly if you use a strong stance to firmly ground yourself.

Belayer positioning. The position of the belayer affects the safety of the climber. If you stand too far away from the wall, the climber can fall directly onto the span of rope that stretches between you and the first clipped bolt. In contrast, the climber can fall on top of you if you are positioned directly against the wall and under the climber. To consider the best spot from which to belay, ask yourself:

Where does the route start and travel?

Where is the first bolt?

What hand will the climber clip with first and where will his stance be at the first bolt?

By answering these questions while bearing in mind your goal of keeping the rope out of the climber's way, you can find the best position from which to belay. Generally, you want to stand relatively close to the wall, off to one side of the first bolt, and not underneath your climber. This will allow you to keep the rope out from under the climber's feet. Once the climber ascends higher than the third or fourth bolt on the route, you can move back from the wall to help you to see the climber's movements and anticipate his needs.

The belayer is positioned close to the wall to minimize the distance from the climber, but stands off to one side to avoid being hit by the climber in the event of a fall close to the ground.

ROPE MANAGEMENT PRECLIMB

After choosing whether or not to anchor and a belay position, uncoil and neatly stack the rope by simply running its length through your hands and letting it form a small pile on the floor at your feet. Be sure to keep track of the end of the rope that is at the top of the stack, as this is the end that the climber will tie in to. Stacking the rope will help you to smoothly feed rope to your climber and minimizes the potential for the rope to form tangles as it is paid out.

BELAY MOTION

The principles of belaying a leader are the same as in top-rope belaying, except that you must provide slack to your climber in addition to taking up rope as she climbs. If you are accustomed to belaying top-roped climbers only, providing slack may feel a bit counterintuitive and will require some practice.

As discussed in Chapter 2, Equipment, there are many different styles of belay devices and the type of belay device will dictate the techniques you use for paying out and taking in slack and for lowering. Tubular belay devices are most often used due to their ease of use, low cost, and light weight. However, the indoor and sport-climbing communities have also embraced the self-locking Petzl GriGri, even though it is much heavier, about four times the cost of a tubular device, and requires a substantial amount of practice to ensure efficient and safe use.

Belaying With a Tubular Belay Device

Paying out slack. As the climber moves away from his last clipped bolt or needs some slack to clip a carabiner, the belayer must feed rope to the climber (also known as giving rope or slack). The climber's speed and the length of rope he requires to clip a bolt will dictate the amount of rope given by the belayer.

To feed out slack, hold the climbing side of the rope with the guide hand thumb up and near the belay device. The brake hand should grasp the brake strand of the climbing rope comfortably away from the body. Grasping with the brake hand with the palm facing down provides a more

ergonomic brake position, but most belayers find a palm-up position to be more comfortable. As the climber needs more rope from the belayer, push rope into the belay device with the brake hand while simultaneously pulling rope through with the guide hand. The finishing position for one stroke of arm movement is with the brake hand near the belay device (but not touching it) and the guide hand extended away from the body. To reposition the hand back into the start of the sequence, hold the brake hand still while sliding the guide hand toward the belay device. As soon as the guide hand has control of the rope and is still, slide the brake hand away from the belay device to the start position. From here, repeat the sequence with the appropriate frequency and speed to keep your climber safe. Short, choppy pulls of rope to the climber can be avoided by paying out full arm-lengths of rope as needed. As with top-rope climbing, maintain control of the brake strand with the brake hand at all times.

As the climber pulls out rope to make a clip, he may have to grab more than one pull to reach the quickdraw. In this case, the belayer should try to match the amount of rope pulled up by the climber. The climber requires special attention from the belayer while clipping, because a fall with rope out can be disastrous. If the climber were to fall with rope out to clip, the belayer can quickly take in slack. As soon as the climber clips the rope into the draw, the belayer should take in the slack to maintain the proper rope drag.

Taking up rope. As a climber moves up toward a clipped bolt or as he downclimbs from a clipped bolt, the belayer must take in the slack that is created. Failure to do so may leave excess slack in the system, which could result in an exceptionally long fall. The motion that is used to take up rope is identical to top-rope belaying (see Chapter 3).

Braking a fall. The major difference between braking a lead fall and a top-rope fall is that lead falls often generate significantly more force than top-rope falls, as the climber is often falling a greater distance. For this reason, and although a climber may use the command "Falling" to warn his belayer to anticipate impact, the belayer must be ready at any time. Even if the climbing is easy and the leader feels comfortable, spinning holds and unexpected slips can catch the team off guard.

Lowering. By clipping the rope in to the anchors at the top of a lead climb, the climber establishes a standard slingshot top-rope system. To bring the climber down, use the same lowering techniques as in top-rope climbing (see Chapter 3).

Belaying with a GriGri

The greatest benefit of a GriGri is its ability to lock the rope during a fall, thus aiding the belayer in braking the system. The GriGri's locking mechanism is similar to that of a car seat belt. If rope is pulled out

This belayer has an athletic stance, allowing him to be mobile and absorb the force of a fall, and he is focused on his climber.

This belayer is inattentive and there is excessive slack in the rope. Do not belay or allow yourself to be belayed in this way!

in a smooth, slow manner, it will slide easily. However, pulling the rope through the device too quickly or with too strong of a pull will lock up the device. Releasing the locked device also differs from a tubular device in that a GriGri has a lever that must be released. In most other ways, using a GriGri is similar to using a tubular device.

Paying out slack. When the climber moves up the wall at a slow or constant rate, feeding rope is the same as with a tubular device. However, to quickly feed rope to a climber, the locking mechanism must be held in a disengaged position. To do this, start with the brake hand holding the brake strand right next to the GriGri with the palm facing up. For the belayer who brakes with the right hand, slide the brake hand against the belay device so the pinky and bottom of the hand prevent the brake-lever arm from locking. Be sure the brake hand maintains control of the brake strand while pushing the brake lever against the body of the GriGri with the bottom of the hand. With the brake lever disengaged, the guide hand can smoothly pull rope to give slack to the climber. Be extremely cautious while pushing the brake lever against the GriGri and only do so while feeding rope. If slack needs to be taken up quickly, the brake hand must be able to pull rope through the device immediately.

Taking up rope. There is no difference in taking in slack with a GriGri compared to a tubular belay device. Because of the increased friction of the rope running though the GriGri, inefficient technique can make taking in rope more difficult.

Remember to pull rope toward the belay device with the guide hand while simultaneously pulling rope away from the device with the brake strand.

Braking a fall. The brake position and act of braking a fall is the same with a GriGri as it is with a tubular device. However, with the GriGri's self-locking mechanism, the force and effort needed by

When paying out slack with a GriGri, the brake hand must hold down the brake lever while still maintaining control of the brake strand. This is not an easy task and requires plenty of practice.

KEY EXERCISE
Learning how to lead belay
The Challenge

Keeping a lead climber safe requires not only vigilant attention on the belayer's part, but also quick reflexes. The lead belayer constantly adjusts to the climber's movements and ultimately prevents a ground fall, while minimizing the climber's flight time.

The Goal

Improve reaction time when feeding out rope, taking in slack, and assuming the brake position without belaying an active climber.

The Equipment

- Harness
- Lead-climbing rope
- Belay device
- Partner

The Setup

In an area with ample floor space, flake the climbing rope and load the belay device. Your partner ties into the climbing end of the rope, facing away from you.

Ground School Lead-belay Exercise

1. With your climbing partner, double-check the setup and go through the commands as if climbing a vertical route.
2. Instead of climbing up a wall, the climber walks away from the belayer, simulating an ascent.
3. The belayer feeds out rope appropriate to the walking speed of the climber.
4. The climber should periodically stop and simulate clipping a quickdraw or downclimbing by walking back toward the belayer. The belayer should react accordingly.
5. At some point, have the climber run forward to simulate a fall.

Considerations

You can perform this exercise with either a tubular device or GriGri.

Practice feeding enough rope so that the climber's forward movement is not limited, but not so much rope that it sags on the ground.

Without a floor anchor, pay special attention to stance. If not, you will be pulled off your feet.

Learn the mechanics of lead belaying with ground school practice.

the brake hand to hold a fall is minimal. This does not mean, however, that you should disregard the importance of the brake hand when using a GriGri. You must still keep your brake hand on the brake strand of the rope at all times.

Lowering. Lowering a lead climber with a GriGri is the same as with a top-roped climber. With the brake hand still holding onto the brake strand, grab the plastic lever on the device with the guide hand and rotate it up until you feel a change of tension against the lever. By pulling back farther than the initial point of tension, the pressure point on the rope opens, allowing rope to slip through the device and lower the climber. When lowering with a GriGri, focus on controlling the climber's descent by using the guide hand on the lever, with the brake hand backing up the descent from the brake strand. Just like with a tubular device, keep the brake arm straight, preventing the hand from creeping up into the belay device. If the climber descends too fast, let go of the lever to immediately stop the climber, but keep the brake hand secure.

Although the GriGri can improve the safety of a climbing team, it is not a substitute for attentive and vigilant belaying. Because the hand motions of feeding rope are different than those used with a tubular device, and because lowering involves more attention from the guide hand, practice and master belaying with a GriGri before entrusting your partner's life to it.

KEEPING THE CLIMBER SAFE

The belayer's responsibilities extend beyond taking in slack, feeding out rope, and braking the climber in a fall. Positioned on the ground, the belayer has a different perspective on the safety of the climber.

Indoors, the belayer is often in a better position than the climber to assess the line a fall will take. Although the climber may control how she falls, the belayer's actions will dictate the length of the fall. One may think that the best fall is the shortest fall, but on overhangs and other protruding features, this is not always the case. For example, if a climber is 10 feet above an overhang, with her last bolt 5 feet below her, falling at this point with a tight belay will slam her into the lip of the overhang. This can be particularly dangerous if the climber's feet clear the overhang but her upper body does not. To prevent this from happening, a belayer might give the climber a bit more slack to ensure that the climber will clear the lip in the event of a fall. The objective of belaying is to catch the climber and prevent a ground fall, so be careful with excess slack.

Communication between the climber and the belayer is essential in keeping the team safe. In addition to the basic commands, it is the belayer's responsibility to let the climber know of potential dangers. Because of a high level of stress and concentration on moving up on the climber's part, potential hazards such as backclipping, Z-clipping, skipping draws, and backstepping the rope can occur unnoticed by the climber. The belayer should communicate with the climber to let her know of these potential dangers, but should do so using a calm, unpanicked manner.

PUTTING THE SYSTEM TOGETHER

Although lead belaying and climbing have been presented separately, the actions of one depend on the other. Working together is essential in safe climbing. Climbers have their own "style" and partners may need to become accustomed to each other. Some climbers clip draws from low positions, requiring the belayer to feed a lot of rope. Others may feel more comfortable clipping at their waist, where the belayer need not feed any rope to clip. Since these differences vary between climbers, attentive climbing and belaying

make for a safer environment. There is no substitute for vigilant and attentive belaying. Climbing gyms afford many social distractions, but the sole purpose of the belayer is to focus on the safety and well-being of the climber.

As with all technical skills, perfect practice is the only way to ensure safety while lead climbing and belaying. Practicing the Key Exercises will better prepare climbers for the decision-making and adversity of lead climbing. Not only should the climber and belayer achieve a comfort level in their roles, but they must also be able to assess their actions and subsequent results. It is not enough to simply "lead and belay" correctly. The ability to logically assess situations and make informed, smart decisions is just as important. Addressing the following points will help the team examine their safety:

	Belayer	Climber
Preclimb	Belay device and rope attachment Proper positioning Anchored Rope flaked Stance Open line of communication	Tie-in point Locating the first bolt Potential clipping holds Assessing the route Open line of communication
During the Climb	Rope management Proper clipping Amount of slack Stance	Rope management Clipping stances Proper clipping Final anchors properly clipped

KEY EXERCISE

Mock leading and belaying

The Challenge

There is little room for mistakes when lead climbing or belaying, and learning how to do either in a situation of live consequences is not recommended. There are many factors involved in minimizing the climber's risk, so mock leading and belaying provides reasonable room for error while learning.

The Goal

To simulate all the components of lead climbing and belaying in the most realistic situation possible. This is also the best scenario to practice lead falls in a controlled environment.

The Equipment

- Harness
- Climbing shoes
- Belay device
- Lead-climbing rope
- Lead-climbing route with top-rope accessibility
- Lead belayer
- Top-rope belayer

The Setup

With the lead belayer, set up to climb the lead route. In addition to tying in to the lead rope, also tie in to the top-rope, managed by another belayer. When climbing the lead route, the top-rope is available for added security, in case the lead climber or belayer has difficulty.

Mock Leading and Belaying Exercise

1. Go through the preclimb check with the top-rope belayer.
2. Go through the preclimb check with the lead belayer.
3. Before climbing, decide which belayer will take and lower the climber.
4. The climber leads the route while on top-rope belay. This situation is "real" in every sense for the entire party.

Considerations

If just beginning to lead climb and belay, the top-rope should be the primary safety rope. Keep the top-rope belay snug, so if the climber falls or needs to rest, he does not take a lead fall.

When comfortable, reach a consensus within the group that the lead belay is the primary safety rope. In this case, the top-rope belay must be loose enough to not interfere with a lead fall.

As a climber, take realistic falls between bolts. Start with letting go with the last bolt clipped near the waist. As you feel more comfortable, take slightly longer falls. Do not skip bolts or take excessive falls

Accidents still happen when taking lead falls while mock leading. Check with the staff at your gym to see if they have any special conditions for taking lead falls.

CLEANING A LEAD ROUTE

After finishing a lead route and safely reaching the ground again, the lead rope travels from the ground, up the wall through the draws, through the anchors, and hangs back down to the ground. To retrieve the rope, either pull the rope down or allow a climber to "clean" the route. When pulling the rope down, start from the end of the rope directly underneath the first bolt. If you pull the rope through the other side, the end will free fall from the anchors, potentially harming someone (or you) as it falls to the ground. If using a figure eight retrace, immediately untie the initial figure eight from the rope so it does not get caught in the anchors.

If opting for a second climber to clean the route, the hanging lead rope is essentially a top-rope with the climber's side of the rope clipped to carabiners. However, the rope must be clipped into the anchors, since these are the same anchors for the second climber to top-rope on. If the lead climber does not clip the anchors, then pull the rope.

The second climber ties in to the end of rope traveling to the first bolt and the belayer attaches himself to the free end touching the ground. For the most part, do not tie in to the free-hanging end of the rope, particularly on steep or wandering routes. Falls will pendulum the climber out of control, endangering him and anyone else nearby. Once set up, the safety checks and commands are the same as for any other top-rope climb. The only difference is that the climber must unclip the rope from each carabiner as he reaches them. Obviously, the anchors remain untouched and the climber should not climb above them. Before pulling the rope through the anchors after the climber finishes and lowers from the route, announce "Rope" to any nearby climbers in anticipation of its free fall from the anchors.

Following a lead climber is a great way to get used to stopping midroute and dealing with quickdraws.

CHAPTER 6

Bouldering

In the past decade, bouldering has taken the climbing community by storm. Whereas bouldering was once thought of as playing around on small rocks on rest days from climbing, it now receives (and demands) the same respect as other genres of climbing. There are international outdoor climbing areas that attract only boulderers, climbing gyms that offer only bouldering walls, and even companies that manufacture only bouldering gear and equipment.

Bouldering's appeal stems from its focus on movement, the little gear needed, and the fact that it can be done solo and has a low barrier to entry. A boulder problem can range from a one-move wonder to a never-ending traverse. In the time spent on a problem, the climber is simply focused on the moves at hand. There are no distractions from a harness or rope, no fumbling with clipping or unclipping carabiners. Success or failure on a boulder problem is often measured by subtle changes in body positioning.

Because of the minimal requirements for safety and performance equipment in bouldering, including that the boulderer does not need a belayer, a beginner can start bouldering within minutes of being introduced to the activity. There are no knots to learn or formal commands to remember. Just you and the wall. However, a new boulderer should be well informed of the risks that come with bouldering. Because of the freedoms that bouldering offers, there are compromises in safety compared to top-rope climbing.

Another advantage that bouldering has over climbing routes is the actual amount of climbing that can fit into a given amount of time. A proficient duo of top-rope climbers may get in a half dozen routes apiece in an hour, whereas a boulderer could theoretically climb nonstop in that same amount of time.

Because bouldering is such an intense form of climbing, there are seldom relatively good rest holds and positions on set boulder problems. Indoor bouldering is also characterized by overhanging walls. These features put more weight on the climber's upper body, creating extremely difficult moves on still-decent holds.

Bouldering could best be described as free-form gymnastics performed on rock faces. The rock provides features and the climber must create a routine to match those features. The physical and mental demands of the two activities have similarities as well. Participants must be able to blend technical skill with strength and balance, while maintaining the mental edge for success and safety.

THE V-SCALE

Because boulder problems are much shorter than roped routes, a lot of punch is packed into such a little bit of climbing. Roped routes are given a Yosemite Decimal System (YDS) grade based on the hardest moves, or crux, of the climb. One of the draws of bouldering is that it takes the hardest part of route climbing and packs it into a few moves right off the ground. Because of this difference, bouldering has its own grading system. There is a rough conversion between the bouldering V-scale and the YDS. In terms of the actual difficulty of moves, the individual moves that elite boulderers are performing are

YDS VS. V-SCALE

YDS	10b	10c	10d	11a	11b	11c	11d	12a	12b	12c	12d	13a	13b	13c	13d	14a	14b	14c	14d	15a
V-SCALE	0	1			2		3	4		5		6	7	8		9	10	11	12	13	14	15

"harder" than what elite route climbers are executing.

As the comparison grading scale shows, the V-scale is obscure below the YDS grade of 10b. This is because the nature of bouldering is climbing difficult moves. The frustration of this discrepancy becomes apparent when bouldering at the V0 grade. A boulder problem of this grade can reflect the hardest moves of a YDS climbing ranging from 5.0 to 5.10b. Some gyms have created their own sub-V0 scale to help climbers choose routes that are more appropriate for their level.

FOLLOWING A BOULDER PROBLEM

Designated bouldering areas and caves are often riddled with holds and have a rainbow of tape on the wall designating specific routes that have been set. Check with the gym staff to see if the colors have any specific meaning, but usually the color choice is arbitrary. The starts of boulder problems are like those of roped routes: hands should start on a specific hold. There is usually a descriptive note at the beginning of the problem that may indicate the grade, a name for identification, and any other pertinent information.

A boulder problem that is set to be climbed by tracking means that the hand- and footholds marked with one tape color are the only ones you can use to complete the problem at the given grade. Any other hand- or foothold is not considered a part of the route.

Jibs, or tiny footholds that are mounted to the wall with woodscrews, are often considered permanent features on the wall. Some gyms may consider them a part of any boulder problem. Every gym is different, so consult with the staff to find out what the setter's intentions are for bouldering. Of course, you can always disregard the established problems and climb on whatever looks like fun, or perhaps just stick to the designated handholds and use any footholds. Remember, climbing is what you make of it.

SAFETY

It is more probable for an indoor climber to be injured from a bouldering fall than from a roped fall. When climbing on a rope, falls are protected by the rope, preventing the climber from hitting the ground. However, with bouldering, every fall—planned or not—results in the climber hitting the ground. Landing off-balance can twist knees or ankles or sprain wrists. Just being in the cave increases the risk of injury, because someone falling on you is possible. Having a flying boulderer land on you is no fun.

The appeal of indoor climbing for bouldering is just the same as for roped climbing. The landing zones in outdoor areas will never be as flat or as cushioned as in a climbing gym, nor will emergency assistance be as close. Even with these controlled features, injury is always possible. In an effort to help minimize the risk of injury consider the following guidelines:

■ Keep bottles and gear away from landing zones.
■ Be aware as a climber and as a spectator.

■ You are ultimately responsible for your own safety.
■ Know your limits.
■ Use a spotter.
■ Learn to fall.

SPOTTING

Gymnasts use spotters during their routines to help safely guide them to the mats in a fall or dismount. Boulderers employ the same tactics since there is minimal protection from a fall. Being a spotter comes with the same responsibilities as belaying. The climber trusts you to have the focus and attention to react quickly and the technical skills to perform your duty properly. Due to distractions of other people around you, being excited for the boulderer, and not being physically

Proper spotting. As the boulderer climbs higher, the spotter steps back some, anticipating the projection of the falling climber.

linked to your climber with a rope, being a good spotter can seem more difficult than being a good belayer.

The primary goal of the spotter is to help direct and slow the climber's fall. A simple step off the wall by the climber may not require much of the spotter. The spotter simply helps the climber regain her balance if necessary. However, a spiraling boulderer pitching from 10 feet up may require the spotter to forcefully direct her toward a bouldering pad while uprighting her so her feet land first. A large part of directing a falling climber consists of the spotter protecting the climber's head, neck, and back by having her land feet first.

A secondary responsibility of the spotter is to make sure that the landing stays clear of obstacles and that the bouldering pads are moved according to where the climber might fall. However, these tasks should only be done if they do not compromise the protection of a falling boulderer. Obstacles should be cleared before the boulderer starts, and the spotter can direct mat placements to other people in the bouldering area.

The best positioning for a bouldering pad (or crash pad) is so that the climber lands in the middle. Landing with one foot on the pad and one foot off results in unbalanced impact and is a recipe for disaster. The pad should always be moved under control. If the pad is moved with a strong jerk and the climber falls and lands on it while the pad is still moving, he can bet on an ankle injury. When putting two pads together, diligently enforce a tight fit between the pads.

Landing with a foot in the gap is another type of disastrous landing.

The ready position for spotting is an athletic stance with the legs shoulder-width apart, if not slightly wider. One foot can be in front of the other, with knees slightly bent to help either absorb the force of the climber or to help push for direction. Both arms should be raised and positioned near the climber's center of gravity. This may range from the hips to the shoulders, depending on the climber's body type. The spotter should position his body between the climber and the ground. If the spotter is not standing close enough to the climber, the falling climber will simply slip though the spotter's arms. The spotter should keep his hands close enough to prevent the boulderer's body from slipping though his hands. The spotter's hands should be positioned so the palms will take the brunt of the climber's force, with the thumbs kept tight to the hand to prevent sprains.

As the boulderer ascends, keep the hands raised and move accordingly. The steeper the climbing, the more probable it is that a falling climber will be in a prone position while falling. Be ready to slow the climber down by contacting him slightly higher than his center of gravity. This will cause the legs to continue to fall and land sooner than the back and neck.

Just like a belayer is ready to react to a climber from the moment he leaves the ground until he returns, a spotter should never let his guard (or hands) down until the boulderer is safely on the ground. A common (and dangerous) mistake is to either stop spotting or let the hands down once the boulderer has reached the top of the climb. In fact, descending is one of the riskiest parts in any form of climbing. A hold could spin or the climber could lose balance and come crashing off the wall. As a spotter, dedicate full attention for the duration of the ascent and descent.

Consider multiple spotters for high-risk bouldering, even in the gym. Bouldering is a very social activity and there are often able bodies to help spot or move bouldering pads. Just make sure that everyone is an experienced spotter. An ineffective spotter is worse than none at all, since the climber has a false sense of security and that spotter may injure the climber, himself, or other spotters.

GETTING DOWN

Since what goes up must come down, part of safety is knowing the ways to get down from a bouldering problem. The safest way to descend is by climbing all the way back down to the ground. If you are climbing at your limit, this may be a problem since you have spent all your energy on the ascent. Look for the biggest holds you can and use them to downclimb. Thoughtful climbing gyms place descent jugs on high bouldering walls.

Jumping down and falling are also options for descent. The difference between the two is that jumping down is a conscious decision and falling is not. When jumping down, check your landing zone. Hopefully, it is a clear area that is at a close enough, comfortable distance. If not,

downclimb a bit or traverse over to a bouldering pad. When landing, slightly bend your legs and land with both feet at the same time. When jumping, avoid any rotation to prevent excess torque on your ankles or knees at impact. As you hit the ground, let your legs bend some more to absorb the force of the landing. On long air time jumps, continue your momentum to carry your upper body all the way down to the ground by rolling sideways.

Note that if you always revert to jumping or downclimbing when the moves get difficult, you will have a hard time pushing yourself and bettering your bouldering skills. Knowing how to fall will provide a comfort level that will let you push your limits.

When pushing your personal performance envelope, falls are often unexpected, due to the amount of focus on the movement at hand. After the realization of falling sets in, try to position your feet below your body, feet landing first and slightly bent, just like jumping down. Try to minimize rotation before you hit the ground. Be careful using your hands for stabilization once you hit the ground. Wrist sprains are a common injury when falling backwards, since a natural reaction is placing your hands behind you to break the fall.

GETTING STARTED

Bouldering can be intimidating. Climbers swinging through the air, falling out of the sky, the steep terrain, and lack of a top-rope can make a bouldering area seem foreign to any climber, new or experienced. If the crowds are intimidating, consider bouldering at off-peak hours, like during a weekday afternoon. You are likely to have the gym to yourself. At the same time, safety in numbers is often true, so try to gather up your climbing partner to go bouldering with you or meet up with some more experienced friends so they can show you the ropes (although technically, there are none in the bouldering area).

REMEMBER SAFETY

As noted before, every time you let go of the wall while bouldering, you will hit the ground at the appropriate speed of gravity. If you are near the ground, this is not a problem, but coming off the wall at 14 feet creates very different risks, even with a team of experienced spotters. Since you are responsible for your own safety, it is important for you to know your limits. Only you know what you are capable (and incapable) of doing. Never assume that someone will spot you. Ask for a spot from someone capable every time you think you may need one. While spotting is deeply ingrained in the outdoor bouldering community, it is not as much a part of the indoor culture due to level and softly padded flooring.

Move the crash pads into an anticipated landing zone. If possible, cover the entire area below the climb. If that is not possible, pad the area below the crux or the higher, more potentially dangerous parts of the problem. Anticipate moves that may carry you away from the wall, like long dynos or sideways lunges. Even with a perfect spot, you can still get hurt.

WHAT TO CLIMB

A beginner to climbing should focus on bouldering horizontal traverses, as opposed to vertical boulder problems. This way, attention can be paid to movement, and the ground is only a short step away. For boulderers with more experience, scope out problems that look interesting and are appropriate for your current ability. For any climber, choose a height that you feel comfortable falling or jumping down from. This may be the top for some climbers or just a few feet off the ground for others. If you have not properly warmed up yet, start with some very easy problems to stretch your muscles and tendons.

If there are not enough routes set at your experience level, there are always modifications you can make to the ones available. To make established routes climbable, consider using all the footholds on the wall while sticking to the marked handholds. This allows you the freedom to place your feet on the most efficient holds for your body type and to maintain proper body positioning. As your bouldering ability improves, try to stay on the designated footholds.

BOULDERING TECHNIQUE

Due to the severely overhung terrain and short bursts of power and high-intensity climbing required on boulder problems, the movement characteristics of bouldering often differ from roped climbing. All of the climbing techniques described in Chapter 4, Movement Technique, are relevant to bouldering, but more advanced overhanging techniques like twistlocks and knee drops are discussed below. Because many of these techniques require full-body involvement, core body strength is especially important in bouldering.

Core strength is defined as the ability to stabilize and control the stomach, lower back, and hips. Steep climbing depends on body positioning and hip placement, and core strength is the connector between tension created with the upper and lower body. The connection between upper-body tension, core tension, and lower body tension is collectively called body tension. When climbing vertical or less-than-vertical terrain, a climber's center of gravity pulls the hips into the feet. On steep overhanging terrain where the climber is in a more horizontal position, gravity pulls the climber's hips down and away from the feet. Because of this, more body tension is needed in steep climbing and bouldering than vertical routes, and this means more core strength.

TWISTLOCKS

Overhanging terrain can be intimidating. However, with some changes in body position and technique, steep terrain can be masterfully climbed with grace and fluidity over brute strength and power.

The most basic technique for steep climbing is the twistlock. The twistlock is a modification of crossing through. If you were to tackle an overhanging wall in a frontal position with your hips and chest square to the wall, gravity would tug your hips down and an incredible amount of force would be required from one arm to allow the other to simply let go and reach up. Although the principle of keeping as much weight over the feet as possible remains true, it must be achieved differently on an overhanging wall by using twistlocks.

Set up for twistlocks by sitting on the ground with your feet in front of you like they are on the wall and your hands out in front of your face like they are grabbing imaginary holds. Pretend you are on a 45-degree overhanging wall. To reach your right hand to a hold, drop your right knee toward the ground between your legs. You should feel your right hip raise off the ground, in turn, raising your right hand a bit higher. This is the twisting motion of a twistlock. What you have achieved by dropping your knee is to bring your center of gravity (hips) slightly closer to your feet and to extend your reach by rotating your body. The final part comes from "locking" off the left arm by bending it just enough for the right hand to grab the hold.

Performing a twistlock is a full-body move. Your toes, fingertips, and everything in between are fully engaged to create enough body tension to keep your hips tight and prevent any body part from sagging.

Since every body part has its job in performing an efficient twistlock, mastering this move takes a lot of practice, concentration, and body awareness.

It is important to use the inside edge of your toes when setting your feet up prior to a twistlock. This enables your body to pivot on your feet for a sufficient twist of the hips once the movement is engaged. The width of your stance also plays an important role in the line between balance and reach. If your feet are wide apart, you generally can maintain a more stable stance. The drawback is that your reach is compromised. Keeping your feet close together gives you maximum height when reaching, but the balance platform is less stable. Of course, the footholds that you actually have available will dictate your stance, but when practicing twistlocks, experiment with different distances between your feet.

Also, it is imperative to keep your arms straight between twistlocks. If your elbow is bent, then the muscles in your arm are contracted, taking the brunt of your weight. That is a sure way to tire quickly. If your arms are straight, the force of your weight is taken by the bones in your arms, rather than the muscles.

For reaching with the right hand, engage the twist by rotating your right knee between your legs. This will push your hip toward the wall. A narrow stance may only need a subtle swivel of your knee to get your hips in place, but a wide stance may require your knee to rotate

Steep terrain resting position

The subtle knee and hip rotation of a twistlock, to start the reach

Midway through the twistlock, reaching and rotating from the shoulders while the hanging arm stays straight

The final phase of a twistlock, bending the hanging arm at the last moment for full extension of the reaching hand

inward until it is pointed at the ground, flexibility permitting. Once twisted, concentrate on pushing your feet out from each other against the holds, rather than straight down. The more you push with your feet, the less body weight your arms feel. Moving up the body, keep your hips tight against the wall. In our example of reaching with the right hand, your right hip should be right up against, if not touching, the wall. Any relaxation in your abdomen will cause your hips to sag from

the wall, making it harder to maintain body positioning.

Your left arm should remain straight for as long as possible. When moving your right hand up, reach with your shoulders. Your left arm should remain stationary with a bend at the shoulder and with the right shoulder reaching for the next hold. The last movement in the twistlock is to break the weighted arm at the elbow, if some extra extension is needed to grab the hold.

When stringing multiple twistlocks together, keep your right arm straight as you weight it. Then, release the lower body twist and move your feet up the wall. You are now in the starting position for twist-locking on the other side of your body.

A TWISTED CHECKLIST

- The inside edge of your feet should be on footholds, allowing rotation.
- Keep your arms straight.
- Rotate the knee on the side of your body that you are reaching with toward your midline.
- Push out with your feet and squeeze your hip toward the wall.
- Reach from your shoulders.
- Lastly, bend the supporting arm that has been kept straight throughout the move.

DROP-KNEE MOVES

Extreme twistlocks require the rotating knee to turn so severely that it can even point down and away from the wall. The benefit of this type of move is maximizing the pressure of the legs pushing out from each other and widening the climber's base of stability. Because of the high torque placed on the ligaments of the knee, this move has a high potential for knee injury. Although quite effective, take care in executing big drop-knee moves.

HEEL AND TOE HOOKS

The key to climbing steep overhangs is straining the arm muscles as little as

A strenuous drop-knee move, where the knee rotates far enough to point toward the ground

possible by weighting the lower body as much as possible. Heel and toe hooks are effective ways of achieving this, since these moves allow the lower body to "pull" instead of push. Heel hooks are most effective when placed in a horizontal line with the hands. Although this requires a certain amount of flexibility, it essentially creates a third hanging point, in addition to the arms. When moving from this position, forcefully pull the hips toward the heel

Resting off a heel hook in anticipation of reaching with the left hand, most of the climber's weight is distributed between the straight right hand and left heel.

Similar to a twistlock, during a heel hook the torso is raised as high as possible before reaching with left hand. Note how the climber's hips are pulled closer to the heel-hooking hold to minimize weight distribution to other parts of the body.

hook with the hamstring muscles. Raising the hips high minimizes the arm reach to the next handhold.

A solid toe hook can also pull the center of gravity over the feet more effectively. Pay special attention to keeping the hooking foot and ankle rigid as the toes and hips are pulled together. A toe hook can be secured by pushing the opposite foot on the same hold. The pushing of the opposite foot and pulling of the toes allows the lower body to "lock" into the hold and is called a bicycle move.

A bicycle move with the left foot pushing and the right foot pulling

KEY EXERCISE
Learning movement through bouldering with other climbers

The Challenge

In roped climbing, there is seldom the chance to climb with more than one other person at a time. Bouldering reveals a more social aspect of climbing and allows multiple participants to climb with, learn from, and help each other. This group game enforces sequencing, visualization, and movement, all on steep terrain in a bouldering environment.

The Goal

Develop sequencing and visualization skills, hold memorization, and hold selection through a group bouldering game.

The Equipment

- Wide amount of bouldering wall space
- As many hand- and footholds as possible
- Climbing shoes
- Between two and six boulderers

The Setup

The bouldering wall should be set with a wide variety of hand- and footholds. There do not need to be any set bouldering problems.

Add-on Exercise

1. The first boulderer starts by choosing and climbing three moves on the wall.
2. The next climber must climb using the same three holds as the first climber, then add three more moves of her own.
3. The next climber performs the previous six moves, and then adds three more.
4. When all the climbers have gone, the cycle repeats with the first climber again.
5. When a climber fails to repeat all the moves and add three more, he is "out." The next climber attempts the same moves.
6. The game continues until one person is left climbing.

Considerations

Gauge the ability of the group. Adding moves that are too hard for most of the climbers does not make the game fun for everyone.

Determine what the goal of the game is before you start. If it is a game of endurance, keep the moves easy and flowing. Training for power will keep the number of moves short.

The more people playing, the longer the problem will get more quickly. Consider only adding two or even one move if you have a lot of climbers.

CHAPTER 7

Performance

The joy and excitement of a new climber reaching the top of a beginner's wall can be just the same as that experienced by an elite climber completing a 5.13. The common thread between these two climbers is the personal challenge the route provides and the satisfaction of rising to meet those challenges. Sometimes, joy of movement is enough, but for a lot of climbers, seeking challenging routes is the draw of climbing.

As a climber's ability improves, different challenges are unlocked and discovered. Improvement is a quest to master an activity and often the desire to improve comes from dedication to and enjoyment of the activity. As with most things in life, the more time, energy, and effort put into the activity, the richer the results. Climbing performance, or the way we function while carrying out the act of climbing, is a product of our investment in time, energy, and effort.

There are many factors that contribute to overall climbing performance. A climber may have impeccable technique but her lack of mental tactics might limit overall performance. Another may be a muscularly strong individual whose sloppy technique is his barrier to improvement. To reach your full potential, physical conditioning, mental approach, and technique must all blend together for optimal climbing performance.

PERFORMANCE PLATEAUS

Although every climber experiences a different learning curve, or rate of improvement, reaching a performance plateau is inevitable. Even the most elite climbers have reached plateaus at the 5.15 grade. Some climbers accept their lack of improvement and continue climbing with the same level of enthusiasm. For these climbers, it is impossible to admit that they will not improve, because at any level, steps toward improvement are always available. Even the most elite climbers have room for improvement. The challenge is in deciding whether an attempt at improvement is worth the time and effort. Advanced climbers must exert proportionally more effort than novice or intermediate climbers for even small gains in improvement. What follows are common reasons for performance plateaus. While the bulk of this chapter is dedicated to solutions, evaluating the reasons for improvement stalls can help you identify the areas needing most attention.

CLIMBING VOLUME

It is common to see a new climber bit by the climbing bug come into the gym nearly every day of the week, climbing several hours at a time. While he may think frequent climbing is the best way to improve, too much climbing does not give the body enough time for rest and recuperation. Conversely, infrequent climbing (e.g., less than once a week) limits continual improvement. What is too much or too little climbing depends on the individual, and can sometimes be a fine line.

TERRAIN

We have a tendency to climb terrain that suits our strengths. For instance, if your forte is steep routes, your route selection gravitates toward routes of that nature. If your movement skills on less-than-vertical climbs are not regularly used, your proficiency on that terrain will decline. Simply put, use it or lose it. Even if being a well-rounded climber is not important to you, to climb well at any grade requires a diverse bag of tricks.

GRADE

Continually climbing on routes that are beyond your current skill level can keep you from learning the proper techniques for the moves at hand. In addition, constant failure on routes that are beyond your limit can create too much frustration, making you question your progress. To improve, a climber's current skill level must be matched with a route to create an appropriate amount of challenge. At the same time, climbing too many easy routes can mentally disengage the climber, eliminating the self-challenge of the activity.

MENTAL APPROACH

Your mental state of mind—either during a climb or the way in which you approach climbing—is a powerful tool that is as trainable as the rest of your body. Goal setting, visualization, and maintaining self-confidence are all mental issues that affect how the body performs. Even how you schedule your climbing sessions significantly affects performance.

BIOMECHANICS

How your body moves and the forces created upon it largely involves climbing technique. Perhaps even more important than learning proper technique and body positioning as a beginner is maintaining proper form throughout your climbing career. While your climbing movement style may not change drastically over time, it is possible to pick up bad habits that can negatively affect improvement. Deterioration in technique by picking up bad habits can change a climber's movement style.

TECHNIQUE

Climbing movement is covered in-depth in Chapter 4, Movement Technique. This factor of performance should be mastered before focusing too much time and effort on the other aspects of performance. Climbing is such a movement-specific activity that learning how to properly travel is the foundation of any climber's success. In addition to performing the technique Key Exercises in this book and mastering those skills, doing so with the guidance of an instructor is invaluable. An experienced technique instructor has the ability to analyze your movement and point out the weak links in your armor. While your belayer or climbing partner can give you objective feedback, subjective pointers may be overlooked. Bad habits are hard to break, so it is important to have your climbing evaluated at the beginning of your climbing career and perhaps biannually to ensure that your technique is up to speed.

Video analysis can be a valuable tool. You probably know more about your partner's climbing technique than your own, since the only analysis of your own climbing movement is subjectively how you feel. You may not realize that you chalk up excessively before every crux, drag your right foot against the wall when your left foot is high-stepping, or that you pump your feet a few times before committing to small footholds. Watching yourself on video along with an evaluation by an experienced instructor gives you an essential perspective on your climbing. If your gym's services do not include video analysis, check to see if you can use your own video camera.

PHYSICAL CONDITIONING

While movement technique is the foundation of climbing performance, the body must be able to perform the task at hand. Climbing-specific fitness, such as hand strength, can limit climbing improvement, but general fitness such as weight management also indirectly affects performance. Even if you know the correct body positioning, physical limitations can limit progress and even lead to injury. The main components of physical fitness for gym climbing are flexibility, muscular strength and endurance, and body composition. Lacking sufficient development in any of these areas can be a barrier to improvement.

FLEXIBILITY AND STRETCHING

A full range of joint, tendon, and muscular motion affects climbing performance and prevents injury. Tight tendons and ligaments limit the body's range of motion, can hinder proper body positioning while climbing, and may increase the risk of injury.

Lower-body flexibility (or lack of it) is often noticed during high-steps, stemming, drop-knee moves, and climbing in the frontal position using the inside edge of the foot. Most climbers do not have problems with climbing-specific upper-body flexibility, although inflexible shoulders can hinder gaston moves. Limitations in flexibility are most apparent where overdeveloped climbing-specific muscles impede nonclimbing range of motion.

Stretching, or moving your joints through a range of motion, improves flexibility. Furthermore, stretching before climbing can improve performance and decrease the chance of injury. It is possible to be too flexible. Excessively flexible climbers are susceptible to joint dislocations primarily in the hip and shoulder sockets.

Flexibility can improve in as little as a month if stretches are performed at least twice a week. Hold all stretches in a static position (no bouncing) that creates muscular tension without causing pain for 30 seconds. Be sure to breathe while holding the stretch. To increase the depth of the stretch, gently intensify the force while exhaling. All the pictured stretches can be done without a partner and cover the muscle groups that are most relevant to climbing flexibility.

Upper Back and Shoulders

Bring your right arm across your chest, bending your arm slightly. Grab your arm with your left hand just above the elbow. Your left arm then pulls to the left,

Upper back and shoulder stretch (Photo by Sue Borchardt)

Chest stretch (Photo by Sue Borchardt)

stretching your right arm. Repeat on the other side of your body.

Chest

Stand with your right arm extended with your hand on a wall, preferably grabbing a large handhold if available. If using a blank wall, place the palm of your right hand firmly against it. To initiate the stretch, keep your arm straight and slowly rotate your chest away from the wall. Keep your right shoulder low while stretching. This also can stretch the biceps. Repeat on the other side of your body.

Fingers and Forearms

This first stretch is an excellent preclimb warm-up to get blood flowing through your

Finger and hand stretch (Photo by Sue Borchardt)

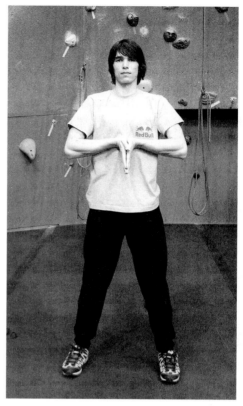

Forearm stretch (Photo by Sue Borchardt)

forearms and to prepare your fingers for squeezing. Hold your right hand in front of your body with your arm extended and palm facing out. Grasp a fingertip with your left hand and gently pull your finger toward your body. After releasing, move on to your other fingers. This can also be performed grabbing multiple fingers of the same hand. Repeat on the other side of your body.

Another stretch is extremely effective postclimb, but is also helpful during warm-up. This stretch can help prevent and relieve blood-filled "pumped" forearms. Place your palms together in front of your body. The heels of your hands should be in line with your elbows. Gently push your hands together while slowly rotating your fingertips down to point toward the ground.

Triceps

Raise your right arm above your head and bend your elbow, reaching your right hand down your back. Grasp your right elbow with your left hand and push your right elbow down and slightly away from your back. Repeat on the other side of your body.

Hips

For the forward lunge, take a long step forward with your left leg, bend your left knee at nearly a 90-degree angle (it should be directly over your left foot, keeping your heel on the ground). While keepin g your right leg straight and your foot pointed forward, maintain an upright posture with your torso. Your right heel does not need to be on the ground. Gently lower your hips down and forward to initiate the stretch.

To improve your turnout, or your ability to rotate your toes and knees away from each other, lay with your back on the floor and legs at a 45-degree bend. Lower your

Triceps stretch (Photo by Sue Borchardt)

Forward lunge (Photo by Sue Borchardt)

Turnout stretch (Photo by Sue Borchardt)

Seated forward bend (Photo by Sue Borchardt)

knees to the outside of your body toward the ground as far as they comfortably move. Allow gravity to further pull your knees toward the ground, opening up your hips. To intensify the stretch, place your hands on your knees and gently push down.

Hamstrings

For the seated forward bend, sit on the ground with your legs extended in front; maintain a slight arch in your lower back with your torso in an upright position. Lean forward from your hips, reaching out with your hands toward your toes and bringing your chest toward your knees. It is important to keep a slight arch in your lower back, so bend your knees enough for your hands to touch your toes.

Neck

"Belayer's neck" is the term used for neck soreness from looking up too much at a climber while belaying. To help prevent soreness, drop your head forward and relax all the muscles in your neck. Then, gently and slowly rotate your head to the side. Stop the rotation when your head is tilted

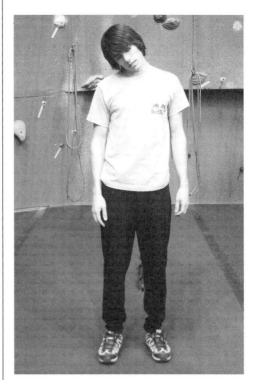

Neck stretch and rotation (Photo by Sue Borchardt)

to the side and then rotate your head to the other side and then back to the middle. The stretch can be intensified by placing a hand on top of your head to gently guide the range of motion.

MUSCULAR STRENGTH AND ENDURANCE

Climbers often state after failing on a route that they "were too weak" or "not strong enough". Most often, deficiencies in climbing technique sap their strength prematurely. However, there are instances in which climbing-specific strength can benefit your climbing. Keep in mind that strength training will make you a better climber only if you have a solid foundation in climbing technique. More strength is the worst substitute for movement skills. Powering through moves will not always work, especially on delicate terrain.

It is also important to understand the difference between strength and endurance. If when attempting a route you lack the strength to perform a single move, strength is the limiting factor. If you fall because your forearms are pumped with so much blood and lactic acid buildup that hand control is lost, then insufficient forearm muscular endurance is to blame. Understanding this difference is essential in identifying your weakness and in training to improve performance.

MUSCULAR BALANCE

Training for muscular strength comprises muscular balance and climbing-specific strength. While developing climbing-specific strength focuses on the pulling muscles of the upper body, every dedicated climber should consider training for overall muscular balance. Climbing, particularly bouldering and steep routes, requires a significant amount of pulling motion with the upper body. This action promotes strength increases in the biceps and shoulders. However, their counterparts, the triceps and chest, remain underdeveloped. This discrepancy in strength between weak triceps and strong biceps make the elbows susceptible to pain while climbing. An underdeveloped chest and strong shoulders can sway posture and lead to injury.

To promote muscular balance, nonclimbing-specific exercises should be performed to strengthen these seldom-used muscles. All of the strength-training exercises shown are performed under body weight, do not require any specific apparatus, and can be done at the climbing gym or at home. Proper form is particularly important with all of these exercises. Improper form renders the exercise ineffective and possibly dangerous. Have your climbing partner critique your exercises or perform them in front of a mirror to ensure sufficient form.

With all of these exercises, perform 2 sets of repetitions to muscular failure. In other words, perform as many repetitions as you can at a steady pace while maintaining good form. Stop the exercises when your form deteriorates. Wait a few minutes, and then repeat the exercise until failure again.

Perform these exercises 2 or 3 times a week. There are a multitude of other exercises that work the same muscles. For an in-depth look at training techniques and methods, consult Eric Horst's *Training for Climbing* and Clyde Soles's *Climbing: Training for Peak Performance.*

Push-ups

Push-ups can be performed anywhere and do not require any special equipment. The resistance from this exercise comes from body weight. To work torso stability, the chest, shoulders, and triceps, lie on the floor with the toes firmly planted on the ground and palms placed just outside the shoulders. While pushing up, the back of the head, back, and legs should be in line with each other. Keep the head facing down to keep the neck from hyperextending. While keeping a straight line between the shoulders and heels through body tension, slowly lower the chest all the way to the floor, touching it if possible.

Placing the knees on the ground is a less stressful modification of the push-up. A narrower hand position, while keeping the elbows close to the body throughout the exercise, places more stress on the triceps. Make push-ups more difficult by placing the feet on a higher platform if necessary.

Dips

Effectively isolate the triceps with dip exercises. Using a stable chair or bench, sit on the very edge of it with the hands placed at the lip next to the hips. The heels of the feet should be on the ground with the legs straight. Push the hips from the bench and straighten the arms. Move the heels a few small steps away from the bench, moving the hips away too. Keep the shoulders high to prevent them from sagging and maintain a slight bend at the elbows. Although dependent on flexibility, lower the upper arms until parallel to the floor. Keep the elbows pointing directly back to isolate the

Push-up starting position (Photo by Sue Borchardt)

Push-up executed (Photo by Sue Borchardt)

Dip starting position (Photo by Sue Borchardt)

Dip executed (Photo by Sue Borchardt)

triceps. Then push back up to the starting position.

The exercise can be made easier by placing the hands and feet on the floor, although the range of motion will be limited. Intensify the exercise by placing the heels on a higher platform, such as another chair.

CLIMBING-SPECIFIC STRENGTH

Inefficient technique can make a climber feel like lack of strength is the limiting factor in climbing performance. However, even with the perfect climbing technique, there comes a time when strength *is* the limiting factor. That strength limitation is often felt in the hands, the point of direct contact with holds.

The common conception is that by just climbing, the hands will get stronger. This is true to a limited extent. The most basic principle in developing strength is that the muscle must be stressed and then allowed to rest. As the muscle adapts to the stress, it becomes stronger and more stress can be applied for additional strength gains. By simply climbing, hand strength will develop and then eventually plateau, since the amount of weight on the hands (body weight) is constant. To add more stress you would have to climb with a weight belt, but this is cumbersome and can negatively affect your technique.

Hangboards. For this reason, a hangboard is an essential training tool for developing upper-body and hand strength and endurance. Given the choice between training with a hangboard or in a traditional weight-training gym, choose hangboards. Hangboards are superior because of their specificity to climbing movement and the strength needed to perform that movement.

Manufactured hangboards are made out of the same material as artificial handholds. These training tools are about as wide as your shoulders and are sculpted with multiple grips, from handlebar jugs to useless slopers. The most basic hangboard has various-sized edges and slopers, while more intricate hangboards have multiple pockets and pinches. Just about every climbing gym in the nation has mounted a hangboard, but their compact size, reasonable price, and mounting ease make them attractive to have at home. It is possible to make your own hangboard by mounting pairs of identical holds about shoulder-width apart. The best place to mount a hangboard is above a door jam, so there is room for your body to comfortably hang freely.

HANGBOARD UPPER-BODY CONDITIONING

The primary upper-body conditioning exercise on a hangboard is a pull-up. The upper body is engaged through a range of motion involving the biceps, shoulders, and back. Because the focus is specifically working upper-body muscles, use the biggest holds. The goal is to work the biceps, shoulders, and upper back to muscular failure, not the hands and forearms.

The more repetitions performed, the more muscular endurance is trained. Modify the exercises for a more strength-oriented workout by adding a weight belt to limit the number of repetitions to less than 5. Your current fitness level dictates whether or not an exercise promotes muscular strength or endurance. For example, if you can perform 8 pull-ups, then that exercise is developing muscular endurance. If your partner can only do 3, his exercises are helping him develop strength.

The following upper-body exercises are listed from least to most demanding. For the best results, meet the first exercise's recommended set before moving on to the next exercise.

Lock-offs

Start with your hands on the largest holds and either jump up or use a spotter or chair to position your chest as high as possible on

Lock-off position (Photo by Dave Hudson)

the board. After shifting all your weight to your hands, maintain the position for as long as possible. Make sure to keep your chest high on the hangboard. Rest for about a minute and repeat again. Work up to 3 sets of 20–30 seconds each.

Lock-off Lowers

Start in the same position as the basic lock-off. As soon as your hands are fully weighted, slowly lower yourself in a controlled manner to full arm extension. If using a chair, make sure it is out of the way during the lowering stage. Step down, rest for about a minute, and repeat again. Work up to 3 sets of lock-off lowers, taking 10–20 seconds to lower.

Pull-up

Start with your hands on the most comfortable holds, arms fully extended and feet lifted off the ground. Raise your chest as high as possible (hand height) and then lower back to the starting position. Focus on stabilizing your body to keep from swinging. For maximum control, pull up on a 2-second count and lower on a 4-second count. Work up to 3 sets of 6–15 pull-ups.

Typewriter Lock-off

Start in the lock-off position, with your chin pulled up above the hangboard. From here, move your chest laterally, touching it (or your chin, a bit easier) to your hand. Alternate touching hands as many times as possible.

Pull-up starting position. The chest is kept high and the arms are nearly straight.(Photo by Dave Hudson)

Typewriter Pull-ups

Typewriter pull-ups are a more difficult variation. From a hanging position, move your chest to the right, pull up, typewriter over to the left, then lower on the left side. Then repeat by moving up the left side, over to the right, then down.

HAND STRENGTH AND ENDURANCE

Climbing would be a different experience if every hold felt like a jug and your hands never fatigued. Hangboard exer-

Type-writer lock-off. Most of the weight is on the left hand, with the right hand stabilizing the body. (Photo by Dave Hudson)

cises for hand strength and endurance might not make those dreams come true, but they will help you hold onto bad holds for longer amounts of time. A majority of the muscles responsible for moving the hand and creating grip strength are located in the forearms, which connect to the fingers via tendons and ligaments. Therefore, forearm and hand strength are closely related. This is why forearm size and definition can help you can pick out the climbers at a party.

The Dead Hang for Endurance

Dead hangs are used for the bulk of hand conditioning. Stand on a chair if you cannot reach the hangboard, then grab a pair of holds. An open hand grip promotes forearm strength more than crimping and is easier on the joints and tendons. Once settled, pick your feet up and hang from the holds for as long as possible. Your shoulders should be engaged, keeping your chest slightly elevated and preventing your upper body from slumping between your arms. Perform 3 sets of dead hangs with about a minute rest between each hang.

Once you can hold on for at least 30

Dead hang for endurance from sloping holds (Photo by Dave Hudson)

seconds, consider using more difficult holds. For each hang, grab a different pair of holds. If you always use the same holds, your hands will develop endurance for that exact position, so vary the grip.

Do 3–5 repetitions of up to 30-second hangs with grip A, a few minutes rest, then 3–5 repetitions of up to 30-second hangs with grip B.

The Dead Hang for Strength

Training for hand strength with dead hangs is similar to training for endurance, but the intensity changes. While endurance hangs are held up to 30 seconds, hangs promoting strength should reach failure in only 5 to 10 seconds. Adding weight increases the intensity of the exercise by overstressing the muscles.

Finding the right combination of hold type and added weight takes some experimentation. A sign of increased hand strength is the ability to hang on for relatively longer amounts of time on the same holds. When you can hang on longer than 10 seconds, add weight. Remember to vary your grip.

Do 3–5 repetitions of up to 5–10 seconds with grip A, a few minutes rest, then 3–5 repetitions of up to 5–10 seconds with grip B.

MUSCULAR STRENGTH AND ENDURANCE IN CLIMBING

The body's muscles initiate movement. For climbing, a minimal amount of strength must be applied to every move. This strength is defined as the maximum

Dead hang for strength. The weight vest turns the endurance dead hang into a strength workout by increasing the intensity of the hang and decreasing the hang time to failure. (Photo by Dave Hudson)

amount of force generated by a muscle or group of muscles. However, there are different aspects of strength as it relates to climbing. A climber has a given amount of strength, but the number of times or the speed with which that strength can be applied greatly affects climbing performance. To improve strength, the distinctions between power, endurance, and anaerobic endurance must be recognized and trained accordingly.

GUIDELINES FOR HAND STRENGTH CONDITIONING
- Long hangs (greater than 10 seconds) to muscular failure develop muscular endurance.
- Short hangs (5–10 seconds) to muscular failure develop muscular strength.
- Alter the hang time by changing the weight and/or the holds.
- Vary the holds to increase your hands' ranges of motion.
- Use an open hand grip to develop forearm strength and decrease the risk of injury.

Power

A powerful climber possesses the ability to perform explosive moves. Defined, power is the amount of work performed divided by the time it takes to perform the work. Using two identical climbers doing the same move as an example, the one who performs the move faster generates more power. Power is often the precursor to dynamic movement, since the initial speed generated carries the climber to the desired holds.

Consider a climber on a route that has a tough move on it, perhaps at a roof. The route, say a 5.10, may contain mostly 5.8 climbing but have a single 5.10 crux move at this roof. If the climber is not able to perform the move, even after ample rest on the rope and using good movement technique, he lacks the necessary power to climb the route.

Developing power. High-intensity climbing through bouldering improves muscular power. The training principle for developing power is short bursts of high-intensity work followed by ample rest. Through bouldering, you can climb a few moves at your limit, then immediately rest.

Many climbers who enjoy roped climbing stay away from bouldering areas, since they do not see themselves as boulderers. However, if lack of power is a weakness, it is impossible to develop it without performing moves at your limit. Climbing for power should come at the beginning of a workout, while the muscles are still fresh and capable of producing 100 percent effort. Take extreme care to properly warm up before a high-intensity bouldering session.

Boulderers training for power should attempt routes two to eight moves long. The rest interval between attempts should be long enough that a forearm pump is not noticeable at the start of the next attempt. An excellent bouldering workout is choosing a problem that you can do a few of the moves on. Attempt the problem and note where you fall (if you do not fall, the problem is obviously too easy). After some rest, get back on the problem at the same spot where you fell to work out the moves. Continue the process until you complete the problem. You can then continue to a new problem, or better yet, repeat the same problem.

Endurance

The ability to generate strength multiple times is muscular endurance. A climber with exceptional endurance never tires. If a climber falls off a route near the top because she simply could not hold on anymore, endurance is the limitation. Most likely, her forearms are pumped and after resting and letting the pump subside, the moves suddenly feel much easier. A 5.10 endurance route could consist solely of 5.9 moves, but the route may be long enough that it feels like 5.10.

Developing endurance. To improve endurance, climb at a low intensity, but for much longer than power training. By performing at a lower intensity, the muscles never work to their fullest capacity and lactic acid production is kept at bay. However, if the intensity of endurance training gets too high, then an overproduction of lactic acid compromises the duration of the workout.

Endurance improves with long bouts of continuous climbing at a low to moderate intensity. For example, climbing up and down an easy-to-moderate route is an excellent way to improve climbing endurance. If possible, try to rest on the route, looking for stems, knee bars, or heel hooks. Choose terrain that allows 10–20 minutes of uninterrupted climbing. This can be awfully boring for a belayer, so consider using auto-belay mechanisms (if provided in the gym) or traverse in the bouldering area. Staying on the wall for that much time can become boring, so consider keeping your mind occupied with technique drills or paying special attention to different aspects of your movement.

Anaerobic Endurance

Between the ends of the power and endurance spectrum lies anaerobic endurance (AE). A route requiring both power and endurance has sections of difficult moves surrounded by moderate climbing or has sustained moves throughout the climb. A 5.10 AE route comprises multiple 5.10 moves. Because of the dual strength demand, it brings out the best (or worst) of both power and endurance climbing.

Developing anaerobic endurance. Whereas power training involves high intensity and short duration, and endurance demands low intensity and a long duration, AE is somewhere in between. Improving AE can be done on roped routes or bouldering. Assessing the true difficulty of each move of a boulder problem is easier than on a roped route, so bouldering is a more accurate means of training for AE. If you do train for AE on routes, look for those with a consistent difficulty of moves.

Consider the 4x4 bouldering workout: Choose 4 problems that you have done onsight. Climb the first problem, wait a rest interval of 2 minutes, then repeat this cycle 3 more times. Follow this with a 5-minute rest then proceed to the second problem. Climb the second problem in the same fashion as the first. Continue with problems 3 and 4. Minimizing the rest intervals between attempts puts more emphasis on endurance. Increasing the difficulty of the problems (and lengthening the rest interval) creates a more power-oriented workout. Performing the 4x4 workout on routes is also possible, but the rest interval significantly increases.

BODY COMPOSITION

A common view of body composition compares the proportion of fat stores, muscle, and bone. Once you stop growing, bone mass is constant, but the amount of muscle and fat tissue can change. Strength gains result from an increase in muscle fiber recruitment and the actual size of the muscle. However, bigger is not necessarily better, since too much muscle can limit range of motion and can be dead weight if in the wrong place.

If you take in more calories than you expend through exercise, these excess calories convert to fat stores. Since fat stores are not a primary source of energy for most gym and rock climbers, this excess is dead weight, constantly pulling the climber down. While it is important that everyone maintain a healthy level of body fat percentage (5–18 percent for active adult males, 16–33 percent for active adult females), excess stores not only limit climbing performance, but impose general health risks as well.

Climbing with a 5-pound weight tied to your waist all the time impedes your strength-to-weight ratio, and excess fat stores are no different than that weight. Using pull-ups to explain strength-to-

weight ratio, the heavier you are, the more strength is needed to perform the exercise. Excess weight alters your center of gravity and hinders body positioning and flexibility. A sensible diet and aerobic exercise are healthy ways to manage body composition.

AEROBIC EXERCISE

Aerobic exercise improves metabolism and burns excess food stores. Continuous exercise that uses large muscles in a rhythmic fashion—such as running, cycling, swimming, or cross-country skiing—burns more calories than stop-and-go activities such as climbing. You can burn excess fat stores and improve blood and oxygen flow with cardiovascular workouts. Even just a little bit of aerobic exercise a week goes a long way in terms of improvement.

Try working out 2 times a week for at least 30 minutes per session. The true path to aerobic fitness is training 3 to 5 days a week at 20 to 60 minutes per session. In terms of total energy expenditure, high-intensity workouts (fast running) for a short amount of time can equal a lower-intensity workout (slow jogging) for a long amount of time. With this in mind, the duration of your workout depends on its intensity.

MENTAL TACTICS

At an elite level of performance, mental strength separates athletes from one another. Physically, they are all quite similar, but the differences in performance are in their mental approach. Elite athletes are not the only ones to use mental training tactics to improve performance. Every climber should pay attention to how the mind affects the body. The central nervous system is a direct physical link between the mind and the body. What you think affects how your body reacts.

Altering your mental approach does not automatically improve climbing performance. The goal of mental training is to create a psychological state that sets the stage for optimal performance. This mental state and the steps to achieve it vary individually. Consider the following aspects that can help create a mental state conducive for climbing performance.

PRECLIMB ROUTINES

Preclimb routines can improve your mental state by telling your mind and body that climbing is about to commence. Something as simple as a couple of specific stretches or retying your climbing shoes can prepare you for the challenge at hand. You may notice that you have already integrated some preclimb safety routines, such as commands with your belayer or spotter. Use these as mental cues to clear your mind and focus on your route or boulder problem.

CONTROLLABLE FACTORS

It is hard to push your limits while worrying about the competency of your belayer, whether or not anyone is spotting, or how well the resole job was done on your climbing shoes. Before actually climbing, deal with any issues that may affect your mental state to limit the amount of mental distractions while climbing. Only so many things can be thought about while climbing, and they should all be directed toward your climbing.

BREATHING

High-intensity climbing often leaves climbers breathless once back on the ground. The breathlessness is not because the climbing was aerobically taxing, like running or swimming. In actuality, climbers tend to hold their breaths or take shallow breaths during heightened states of arousal or physical exertion. The breathlessness climbers experience hinders performance by limiting oxygen flow and increasing muscular tension throughout the body.

Rather than simply trying to remember to breathe, make a concerted effort to take a few abdominal breaths when resting or chalking up on a climb. Start with a complete exhalation, contracting the stomach to squeeze all the air out. The next breath should start by filling the lower abdomen with air and continue the breath into the chest. After a few breaths, the body will be more relaxed, oxygenated, and ready to climb.

MUSIC

Directing your psychological state can be done through music. Just like upbeat, rhythmic tunes make you want to dance and lullabies put a baby to sleep, music can have a similar impact on your climbing. If you are bringing the stresses of work with you to the climbing gym, consider reducing your tension and arousal state by listening to something that puts you in a soothing mood. It is no coincidence that climbing gyms pump out upbeat tunes from their stereos.

MAINTAINING A POSITIVE APPROACH

There is a saying that "whether you think you can or can't, you're probably right." This demonstrates the power of positive thinking and permeates all aspects of life, not just climbing. Maintain a positive approach to climbing at all levels. From having the confidence to set lofty goals to believing that the next handhold can be reached, a positive look at the end result will affect the outcome. A pessimistic view of climbing and your abilities will hurt your performance and, ultimately, your enjoyment of the activity.

VISUALIZATION

Visualization, or developing mental imagery of your climbing, is a powerful tool that can significantly affect climbing performance. Seeing yourself perform at a desired level or executing moves in your mind convinces the body that movements are possible, if not likely.

When attempting to climb a route onsight, visualization depends on the ability to sequence the moves of a climb. If the route is incorrectly sequenced, then visualized incorrectly, you may be setting yourself up for failure. For sections that appear tricky, visualize alternative moves just in case the primary sequence proves impractical. Identifying difficult or tricky moves and then mentally rehearsing them with perfect climbing technique can be done with external or internal imagery.

External Imagery

Picturing yourself on a route as if watching yourself on a video that had been taped with the camera facing the wall is an external approach to visualization. In practice, step back from the route so you can see as much as possible. As you look at the route, visualize yourself standing on the ground, starting with your preclimb routine. See yourself starting to climb in real time and try to go through the entire route in a continuous manner from top to bottom. Picture everything that may happen; clipping carabiners on a lead climb to rest positions, downclimbing and trying different options at the crux, all the way to clipping the anchors. Pay attention to parts of the visualization that become fuzzy or broken. This often indicates an unclear section of the route.

The benefit of external visualization is seeing yourself in relation to the entire route and as successful prior to onsight attempts. With enough external imagery practice, you will develop a clear understanding of your spatial awareness relative to the route. This is helpful in gauging the distance between holds and whether or not you will be able to reach them.

Internal Imagery

Visualizing the climb from an internal approach allows your body and mind to prepare for the climb. Imagine the climb through your own eyes (or on video with the camera placed on the top of your head), as if you were on the route. Be aware of how close the wall will feel to you on different moves, what that next foothold might look like when you are looking down and trying to step on it, or how far the quickdraw is from your head when you are scrunched up in the roof and trying to clip it. If done right, and backed up with external body awareness, you should be able to "feel" the moves before you actually get on the route.

Internal imagery is a key to redpointing success. Because you have already attempted the route, the difficult moves have been identified. For example, perhaps you have been falling on a move that requires a strenuous twistlock and a long reach with your left hand. You have done the move a few times by itself, but fall every time you attempt the entire route.

Mentally rehearse these moves sitting or reclined in a comfortable, quiet place with no distractions. Physically disassociate yourself from the high-energy climbing gym or bouldering cave. Close your eyes and focus on relaxing all the muscles in your body. Start with your head and work all the way down to your feet. Once relaxed, visualize yourself in a comfortable position just before the strenuous twistlock on your route. See yourself climbing up to the crux, paying attention to your body

Mental imagery can be used to help figure out sequences after falling.

relative to the route, like how close your hips should be from the wall, where the footholds are, or how much weight is on your right hand. Make sure your breathing is smooth and controlled. Now, start to move through the crux, focusing not only on how the moves look from your perspective on the route, but also how your body feels. Feel the twist as your left hip rotates toward the wall, the pressure on your toes as they push in opposition through the roof, and reaching for the hold with your left shoulder.

One of the significant factors of mental rehearsal is the ability to focus on the task at hand. You may visualize the crux moves then realize that the grocery list or taking the cat to the vet has crept into your thoughts. Start small, as with focusing on the crux moves of the route. As your ability to focus improves, mentally rehearse longer sections of the route.

GOAL SETTING

Goal setting is a valuable step toward improvement. If you do not know the destination, it is difficult to plan the journey. Partially due to the grading scale in climbing, most climbers define improvement as climbing routes or boulder problems at progressively harder grades. However, improvement can also be aspects of climbing, such as feeling more comfortable lead climbing, getting into the gym more often, or participating in a climbing competition. Whatever your form of improvement is, attaching a measurable outcome to it will help you more easily see the steps towards success. When planning these types of big-picture, long-term goals, think of what you would like to achieve. Setting long-term goals can help keep you focused on the ultimate task.

Short-term goals are the building blocks in achieving long-term success. By providing achievement steps that are appropriate to your current skill level, short-term goal success provides a (relatively) instant gratification that promotes seeking your long-term goal. If one of your big-picture goals is to lead 5.10 in the gym and you are currently a 5.10 climber on top-rope with new lead skills, build solid lead-climbing skills as the first step, work your way through the easy and moderate grades as a leader, and then tackle 5.10 on lead. The sequence of goal setting is to continually break down the goals into the smallest pieces that can be easily managed and achieved. That way, you line your path to success with bite-sized tasks.

SCHEDULING AND PERIODIZATION

If a climber came into the gym twice a week, every week, for a year, and climbed eight routes every time of about the same grade, he would improve some, but then his performance would plateau. Not only that, but climbing the same workouts in such a monotonous fashion is so boring that he may lose interest in climbing altogether. Periodization training, or variations in intensity, specificity, and volume of training, is a key element when training for climbing. Some climbers may periodize their training to coincide with an outdoor climbing road trip, the summer season, or a competition. Others may periodize their training around a specific goal. A periodized training cycle is recommended for climbers who already have developed sound climbing technique and whose performance gains have reached a plateau.

A periodization cycle is designed to allow the climber's performance to peak at certain times or events, often coinciding with set goals. Because the timeline of attaining that goal may be a week to several years, the scope of a periodization could cover that same time range. A long periodization cycle consists of smaller cycles that are repeated and altered to meet the desired outcome. A common cycle is 12 weeks. This is a long enough cycle to make a significant difference in climbing ability, but not too long that the climber loses interest or becomes too fatigued. In addition, four of these cycles conveniently fit into a year, along with some rest time. Within a 12-week cycle are several smaller cycles, designed to work on the components of power, endurance, and anaerobic endurance.

WEEK 1: REST AND ASSESSMENT

The first week of a new training cycle often immediately follows completion of a previous cycle, so use this time for rest and recuperation. Do some climbing just for fun, without any concern for "training." If you really need a break, do not climb at all.

Climbers looking for serious improvement should consider performing a physical assessment at this time. Having quantifiable data on flexibility, muscular strength and endurance, and on body composition is valuable in detecting improvements when taken over time (in this case, every 12 weeks). For safety and accuracy in assessment, use a personal trainer to help measure the following physical components of performance.

Flexibility

Hip turnout. While standing and keeping your legs straight, record the number of degrees that your toes turn out away from each other while your heels stay together.

Sit and reach. This is a standard flexibility test that every personal trainer should be familiar with. While seated on the floor with your legs extended out in front, lean forward from your hips, reaching as far as possible with your hands. If your fingertips do not reach your toes, measure the distance as negative. If your fingertips reach past your toes, measure that distance as positive.

Leg span. Starting in the same position as the sit-and-reach test, spread your legs apart as far as possible, keeping your legs straight. Measure the distance from inner ankle to inner ankle.

Muscular Strength

One repetition pull-up. Record the maximum amount of weight you can add to your body while still performing one pull-up. If you cannot do a pull-up, record the shortest distance between your chin and the bar during the pull-up.

Five-second hang. Record the maximum amount of weight you can add to your body while hanging on holds for at least 5 seconds. Use an open hand grip. The same holds must be used for each assessment.

Muscular Endurance

Pull-ups. Record the number of pull-ups performed in sequence. If you cannot do a pull-up, record the shortest distance between your chin and the bar during the pull-up.

Lock-offs. Record the amount of time that you can hold a lock-off position.

Body Composition

Body-fat percentage. Have a personal trainer measure and calculate your body-fat percentage.

Weight. In minimal clothing, use a scale to record your body weight.

WEEKS 2–4: ENDURANCE CLIMBING

In any physical activity, endurance is the base upon which all else is built. Since developing endurance involves high volumes of low- to moderate-intensity climbing, the occurrence of injury is less likely than in training power. This is especially important at the beginning of a training schedule, when your body is adapting to the physical demands of training. The bulk of climbing during this 3-week session is climbing at or below your onsight grade. The more climbing done in this part of the cycle, the more fit you will be during the transition to anaerobic endurance and power-oriented climbing.

WEEKS 5–7: ANAEROBIC ENDURANCE CLIMBING

Rather than jumping head first into high-intensity climbing after developing an adequate base of endurance, slowly add harder climbing into your training mix. If training for route climbing, add some

bouldering sessions to change the intensity of your workouts. Alternate higher intensity climbing sessions with endurance-oriented sessions.

WEEKS 8–10: POWER CLIMBING

With a foundation of endurance, mixed in with some anaerobic endurance from the last 3 weeks, now is the time to increase the intensity of your climbing while decreasing the volume. Because you are climbing harder routes than the previous cycle segments, decrease the number of routes and increase the amount of rest taken between routes and climbing days.

WEEK 11: TAPERING

The past 9 weeks have been spent training your body to climb better. A well-rested mind and body will improve the chances of peak performance the following week. High-intensity climbing peaked in the power-climbing segment, so decrease the intensity during the taper week and keep the volume to a moderate level.

WEEK 12: PEAK PERFORMANCE

All the hard work is done and this is the payoff week. This 12-week cycle will provide about a week of peak performance. If your peak-performance goal is at the end of the week, be sure to extend the previous taper week to avoid prolonged inactivity.

A CLIMBING SESSION

The smallest component of a climbing periodization schedule is a single climbing session. Just like with an overall periodization cycle, the order and blend of intensity, volume, and specific exercises mold performance. Within a climbing session, warming up, working on technique and skill, performing a focus set, and cooling down all contribute to a meaningful workout designed to help achieve climbing goals.

Warming Up

The tone of a climbing session is set at the warm-up. An improper warm-up can leave you feeling stiff while climbing and can increase the risk of injury, while an adequate warm-up prepares your body for the rigors to follow. The primary functions of warming up are to elevate body temperature and to lengthen the muscles and ligaments, which decreases the risk of injury and can help improve performance. A warm-up is comprised of general and climbing-specific components.

An example of a general warm-up is stretching, calisthenics, or a cardiovascular activity such as running. While these activities are not performed while climbing, doing them prior to your workout improves general blood flow and muscle temperature. An aerobic preclimb workout is not only an adequate warm-up, but also helps weight management. Perform the stretches described earlier in this chapter as well, paying special attention to any muscle groups that may be exceptionally tight or sore.

Easy climbing is the climbing-specific component of warming up. Climb a route below your current onsight level. If you onsight 5.10, consider warming up on a 5.7 or 5.8. During the climb, focus on moving slowly and in control. Gently overexaggerate moves like twistlocks or weight shifts for an extended range of motion that will further increase flexibility. Since the climb is easy, take plenty of time completing it while focusing on footwork and body positioning.

A climbing-specific warm-up avoids the dreaded forearm "flash pump." When a climber grips holds, the hands constantly squeeze and relax, an action initiated by the muscles in the forearms. As the hand squeezes or weights a hold, byproducts of the muscle contraction (lactic acid) develops in the forearms. Because the muscle fibers have contracted, cutting off the blood from leaving the arms, the lactic acid builds. Enough lactic acid buildup leaves the forearms pumped and unable to properly contract and relax the hands. Easy climbing warms up the forearms by allowing a gentle contraction and relaxation cycle, preparing the muscles for more intense gripping later. Once a climber gets a flash pump by climbing too intensely without warming up, the detrimental effects can stay with the climber for the rest of the day.

Skill and Technique Refinement

Deliberately working on climbing skills and techniques is the fastest way to improvement. Because your body is not yet tired and your mind is still fresh, learn and reinforce new skills at the beginning of workout sessions. If working on movement skills, now is the time to practice Key Exercises, have a trainer evaluate your movement, or to experiment with new types of moves. This is also the time to practice technical skills, such as lead climbing or belaying or spotting. Working on skill and technique is not imperative to every climbing session, but if you do choose to work on them, do so right after the warm-up.

Focus Set

This is where the "just climb" part of the climbing session fits in; a focus set is the actual climbing you do during a session. Depending on your goals, the focus of a climbing session can range from having fun with friends to working on bouldering power to lead-climbing endurance. It is a good tactic to have an idea of what you would like to accomplish in your time in the gym. Not having a plan is acceptable, just as long as you at least acknowledge that this is what you want to do. Improvements in power, endurance, or anaerobic endurance fit into the focus component of the climbing session. The focus set can also be the time to redpoint projects or push onsight climbing skills.

Cool Down

Just as important as the warm-up, cooling down is the buffer between maximum exertion and muscle relaxation. Abruptly ending an intense climbing session by simply walking out of the gym can inten-sify soreness and limit recovery the following day. Stretching is ideal for cooling down, along with climbing a few easy routes. Keep in mind that the increased blood flow of aerobic activity after climbing helps flush out metabolic toxins left over from climbing. An excellent time for strength training for muscular balance is after the cool-down session.

SAMPLE IMPROVEMENT SCHEDULES

The following are suggested workouts for novice, intermediate, and advanced climbers. The profile for each climber includes current climbing ability and then a description of what the climber should focus on for climbing improvement. The sample schedule shows how much time should be spent warming up, working on skill, technique, and strategy, climbing a focus set, and cooling down for both endurance and power-oriented workouts.

Novice Climber

This climber is new to the activity, consistently onsighting 5.7 and working on completing routes in the 5.9 range. Time dedicated to climbing is twice a week with about 2 hours per session. As a beginning climber, the focus is on overall climbing techniques. Pay special attention to learning efficient climbing habits. Do not worry about "training," just climb as much as possible while paying attention to good form. Take plenty of rest between climbing days to avoid injury.

NOVICE WORKOUT CHART

Workout Stage	Endurance-oriented Sample	Power-oriented Sample
Warm-up (15 min)	Stretching; 5.4, 5.5, 5.5	Stretching; light bouldering; traversing
Skill and technique (45 min)	2 to 4 Key Exercises done multiple times to facilitate learning	2 to 4 Key Exercises done multiple times to facilitate learning
Focus set (45 min)	Pyramid workout of 5.6, 5.7, 5.8, 5.7, 5.6	Work as many 5.9 routes as time (and energy) allows, repeating the crux sections a few times to get them "wired"
Cool-down (15 min)	5.5, 5.4 (keep it smooth); stretching	5.6, 5.5, 5.4; stretching

Intermediate Climber

This intermediate climber consistently onsights 5.8 routes and some 5.9s. At the verge of redpointing 5.10, two sessions a week are dedicated to climbing in the gym, sometimes with a third. Climbing sessions last from 2 to 3 hours. Having a solid foundation in climbing movement, this climber is beginning to recognize his strengths and weaknesses. He is also

INTERMEDIATE WORKOUT CHART

Workout Stage	Endurance-oriented Sample	Power-oriented Sample
Warm-up (15 min)	Aerobic workout prior to warm-up (additional 20–30 min); 5.6, 5.7, 5.7	Stretching; 5.6, 5.7, 5.8
Skill and technique (45 min)	Work on overhung climbing and bouldering technique; use ample rest to keep from becoming too tired	2 to 4 Key Exercises done multiple times to facilitate learning
Focus set (45–60 min)	In a given amount of time, complete as many 5.8/5.9 routes as possible; consider climbing two routes in a row before switching with the belay	Work on powerful moves through bouldering; start with easy problems and work up to harder ones; after the first attempt, just work on the crux moves
Cool-down (15 min)	5.5, 5.4 (keep it smooth); stretching	5.6, 5.5; finish with an aerobic workout (additional 20–30 min)

realizing that relative inactiveness outside of climbing has him pulling more weight up the wall than he would like. His barrier to entry into 5.10 is the inability to perform the crux moves, while the rest of the route feels comfortable to him.

Advanced Climber

The advanced climber has a solid foundation in climbing movement. She can onsight 5.10 and wants to break into climbing 5.11 onsight. She can invest 2- to 3-hour climbing sessions 2 to 3 times a week. Her onsight plateau at the 5.10 range is due to minor technique flaws or lack of physical conditioning (i.e., flexibility, strength, body composition).

At this level of performance, a lot of effort must be exerted to make even small gains in performance. The climber should set specific goals, like redpointing a particular route in a certain number of days or weeks. She should identify weaknesses and deliberately work on them. The volume of climbing for this person is similar to the intermediate climber, but the intensity is higher.

ADVANCED WORKOUT CHART

Workout Stage	Endurance-oriented Sample	Power-oriented Sample
Warm-up (15 min)	Aerobic workout prior to warm-up (additional 20–30 min); stretching; 5.7, 5.8, 5.9	Several easy boulder problems (less than V1)
Skill and technique (45 min)	Identify technical weaknesses, choose exercises to work on them (e.g., the No-hands Traverse Key Exercise in Chapter 4)	Identify technical weaknesses, choose exercises to work on them
Focus set (45–60 min)	Climb a route at or below your onsight level; downclimb an easy route, then reclimb original route; switch with your partner and then climb again; repeat this for the duration	Complete a 4x4 bouldering workout of V3, V3, V2, and V2; allow 3 min rest between each attempt and an additional 5-min rest before starting a new problem
Cool-down (15 min)	Several easy boulder problems (less than V1); stretching	5.7, 5.6, 5.5; finish with an aerobic workout (additional 20–30 min)

CLIMBING PARTNERS

We all learn movement skills in different ways. Sight is most often used to gather information about and to learn movement skills. With this in mind, who we climb with can affect personal improvement. If you are the most accomplished climber in your regular climbing group, your friends have the advantage of seeing how you perform moves or can take advice from you on their projects. It may be flattering to have your friends hold your climbing in high regard and always come to you for help, but your own improvement may suffer. Take time to climb with people that you can learn from. Of course, this does not mean leave your friends because they do not climb the grades you do. After all, who you climb with is an integral part of the experience. Nor should you climb with people who simply climb harder routes than you. Instead, seek climbers who have performance traits such as excellent technique on technical terrain or a strong mental game. Perhaps you and your climbing posse always choose overhung terrain. A different climbing partner may have other preferences than what you are used to.

Take time to learn about your (potential) climbing partner's goals, to see if the two of you are compatible. If she is an antisocial climbing machine who will not settle for less than twenty hard routes in a climbing session and you just want to climb a few easy routes, keep looking. Even if the partner in question has passed his belay test, make sure that you feel comfortable having that person as a climbing partner.

NONCLIMBING ACTIVITIES

Nonclimbing activities that work on the flexibility, muscular strength, and stability required by climbing can improve climbing performance. For instance, dancing can improve dynamic balance and can even provide an aerobic workout. Gymnastics requires similar muscular demands as climbing. Pilates focuses on core body strength. Yoga improves flexibility, postural alignment, total body muscular stability, and even mental grounding. Because of the similar physical and mental demands and benefits of yoga and climbing, it is common for gyms to offer yoga classes. By engaging in physical activities other than climbing, your mind and body remain balanced against any rigors encountered.

PUTTING IT ALL TOGETHER

A multitude of factors contribute to climbing improvement. From the partners you choose to how much stretching you do before a climb, or from the hangboard workouts to aerobic training, it all makes a difference. An eager climber may want to overhaul his current climbing routine and change every aspect. This is simply impossible. By changing too many aspects of the activity, the initial experience is altered and the allure of climbing is no longer the same. If you alter too many factors, it is difficult to determine which of the variables actually made the difference in performance.

If you desire to improve your climbing by taking steps to higher performance, change your approach one aspect at a time. Climbing 3 times for 3 hours *and* aerobic exercise 5 times for a half hour each workout *and* strength training 2 times a week *and* a structured yoga class every week will leave you no time to enjoy the other things in life and will almost guarantee injury and fatigue.

Start by improving the aspect of climbing that is your weakest link. For some people, that may mean going back to the basics of movement technique or for others, improving endurance. Do not allow training to cause you to lose sight of why you climb. If what you are doing is not fun, then perhaps you should reconsider your goals. If you are not having fun, then what is the point?

COMPETITIONS

Most climbers say they enjoy the internal competition that climbing creates within them. That is, the body and mind have limitations and the climber's challenge is to break those boundaries in search of self-improvement. However, with the social construct of organized competition, performance is displayed publicly and athletes' performances are compared to each other. Organized competitions have developed within rock climbing, providing not only a platform of comparison, but also serving as a celebration of the sport.

A majority of climbing competitions (often referred to as comps by those in the know) are held on artificially built climbing walls with set routes. Most of them are held in gyms, but some are on walls constructed outdoors for increased spectator appeal. The routes required for competition must match the abilities of the competitors. It is too difficult to find routes of the exact grade on real rock without scarring the environment.

SPEED CLIMBING

The rules of a speed-climbing competition are straightforward: the fastest climber to the top wins. Two climbers compete head to head on respective top-rope routes. A competition may have several rounds of climbing, where the winners advance to the next round. If the climbers are not climbing on identically set routes, they may race each other twice, each having a chance on the other route, and the cumulative time will be recorded. Speed-climbing competitions are not very popular on a local or even regional level, but such events are included in international and national climbing competitions.

The aerobic demands of speed climbing is greater than that of bouldering or route climbing. Fluid, dynamic movement is essential for this fast-paced climbing, along with the ability to quickly sequence moves. A technical consideration for speed climbing is that the standard method of belaying is too slow to keep up with the slack generated from a speed climber on top rope. The belayer must modify the belay technique to reel in slack fast enough for the climber.

ROUTE CLIMBING

Route-climbing competitions are also called difficulty competitions. The first international competition was organized in Europe in the mid-1980s, with an international series shortly thereafter, followed by a large interest in the United States. However, the spirit of difficulty comps waned toward the late 1990s as climbers lost interest and embraced a more participant-friendly bouldering format.

More formal difficulty comps call for the competitors to wait for their turn to climb in an isolation (iso) zone. This zone prevents the climber from seeing the routes, or even from coming in contact with anyone who has. Advanced climbers almost always climb on lead, but less advanced climbers may climb on top-rope. When called to climb, the climber truly makes the attempt onsight, with no prior knowledge of the route. Each hold on the route is worth a certain point value. The higher the hold is on the route, the greater the number of points. The climber is then scored on the highest hold reached. The attempt must be completed within a certain amount of time, but that usually does not affect the climber's performance.

A multiple-round format is popular, where to reach the final round, a climber must pass through a semifinal or even a qualifying round. Variations of difficulty comps may allow the climbers multiple attempts on routes, or the number of routes attempted by each climber may vary. More casual, local difficulty comps may integrate bouldering or reject holding climbers in isolation to make for a more social atmosphere. Because difficulty routes require a lot of wall space, take a long time to set, and allow for only a few competitors to climb at a time, bouldering competitions are the newest wave in climbing competitions.

BOULDERING

Along with the bouldering boom of the late 1990s came bouldering comps. These competitions are merely extensions of the energy and camaraderie that has evolved within bouldering culture. Bouldering comps are run in two formats, World Cup–style and redpoint events.

World Cup–style events are molded from a more formal international format. Similar to difficulty events, climbers wait in isolation until their turn to climb. They are given a certain amount of time (around 5 minutes) to complete the first problem. The competitor may attempt the route as many times as desired. The highest point reached is scored, just like in a difficulty event, along with a deduction in points relative to the number of attempts. The climber then enters a rest period, and then attempts the next problem. This true test of power and endurance is a grueling format. However, with multiple climbers attempting different routes at the same time, it makes for a quite an event for spectators.

The camaraderie and peer support of bouldering competitions can elevate your climbing to new heights.

Redpoint-style bouldering competitions are most popular, with hundreds of events at the local, regional, and national level held each year. To set up for a redpoint comp, the gym sets several dozen boulder problems from extremely easy to impossibly hard throughout the gym, giving each problem a point value. The more difficult the problem, the greater point value it receives. Participants climb for several hours, attempting whichever problems they choose. Attempts and ascents are marked on a scorecard. The comp organizers determine how many problems will be scored (generally four to seven) and a

climber's total score is the sum of his or her hardest problems. This format is participant-friendly, since novice climbers compete right along with elite performers and the atmosphere is similar to that of a high-energy bouldering session.

Preparing for a Bouldering Comp

With the number of bouldering competitions increasing every year, chances are your climbing gym will host one. Whether or not you define yourself as competitive or even as a boulderer, consider participating. The crowd and enthusiasm is enough to give you that extra edge and you may find yourself climbing harder than usual. The following tips will help you prepare for a redpoint-style event:

If possible, preregister for the event. By doing so, you commit to participating and allow your psyche to prepare for the comp.

Leave yourself enough room to check in and perform a proper generalized warm-up on the day of the event. Bring your own food and drink.

For your first couple of problems, climb something that you know you can easily do. It does not matter if they are the easiest problems. Climb them slowly, trying to maximize the climbing-specific warm-up.

When you are sufficiently warmed up, look for climbs that:

- Look fun
- Look challenging
- Cater to your strengths (e.g., steep, vertical, crimpy, slopey)
- You might be able to climb onsight

If you manage to do a climb on the first try, rest and try a climb that is a bit harder.

If you do not finish a climb, consider how doable the problem is. If you think you can finish it, give it a few more attempts, but do not exhaust yourself on just one problem. It is all right to pass up a problem in search of others. You can always come back to the problem later.

Before attempting a problem, try to watch other climbers first. Look for tough spots, alternate sequences, or tricky moves. Try to learn from other people who have a similar climbing style to your own.

If you can only remember one thing while you are climbing, "Keep moving." If you can remember two things, then "Look at your feet" is the other.

You probably have many hours to climb during the competition. At some point, take your shoes off and place yourself away from the climbing area to eat and rehydrate. It is important to take yourself away from the action to rest a bit.

Have fun!

STAYING HEALTHY

The best step to staying healthy is avoiding injury. Take the following measures into consideration to help stay out of harm's way. When (not if) you do sustain a climbing injury, seek professional assistance for prompt rehabilitation. Also remember that staying healthy is not simply avoiding injury. While injury impedes climbing progress, staying healthy is the platform that allows for climbing improvement.

AVOID OVERTRAINING

When training for climbing performance, high-intensity workouts can decrease performance for the following 12–36 hours, depending on the intensity. This is a natural reaction, as your body goes through a recovery cycle from the beating it just endured. If you do not allow enough rest between each training bout, then your body can never fully recover. Symptoms of overtraining can include a constant sense of fatigue, a general feeling of heaviness, or even loss of appetite.

LISTEN TO YOUR BODY

Whoever came up with the saying "Pain is only weakness leaving the body" probably did not get very far. Pain is the body's way of telling the mind that something is wrong and needs to be addressed. Even nagging discomfort, of maybe a finger tendon or elbow, will not go away on its own. Of course, the immediate remedy for pain is to stop performing the action that aggravates the injury. But from there, climbers not only need to listen to their bodies, but also need to help them recover. Even minor discomforts can escalate to debilitating pain, so get checked out by a doctor if rest does not significantly improve the problem. Do not climb through pain. You will only make your injury worse.

Properly Fuel and Hydrate

High-energy climbing sessions are often fueled by excitement and fun (and perhaps vast quantities of caffeine), rather than by food and water. If you are hitting the gym after work, eat something before or during your climbing session. If you do not, your body simply will not be able to keep up with your demands. Hydration is another issue gym climbers tend to overlook. If you climb while dehydrated, the risk of injury and muscle cramping increases. In a 2-hour climbing session, drink at least 1 liter of water.

Gradual Reentry

Taking a break of one to several weeks from climbing can rejuvenate your body and refresh your mind, but the longer the break, the more susceptible you are to injury after reentry. While climbing-movement skills may not be affected by the hiatus, muscles and tendon strength, along with joint range of motion, will have decreased. So, when reentering the sport, the difference between what your mind tells your body to do and what it can actually handle can result in injury. After any break, gradually increase the intensity of your climbing. It is impractical to expect to pick up where you left off.

Evaluate High-risk Moves

Harder climbs can require new body movement. High-risk moves, like shallow finger pockets, high gastons, or severe drop-knee moves should be performed with caution. Listening to your body and falling at the first sense of injury is the better alternative to doing the move and blowing out your knee. Also, climbing to exhaustion increases the risk of injury, since weak muscles lose their ability to stabilize the body.

Glossary

aerobic exercise Cardiovascular activity such as running, swimming, or biking.

anaerobic endurance The ability to generate high-intensity strength multiple times.

arête Outside corner feature of a climbing surface.

auto-belay Indoor top-rope belay method using a mechanical device that takes in slack as the climber ascends and that automatically lowers the climber to the ground after she comes off the wall.

backclipped An incorrectly clipped quickdraw that can potentially unclip if the rope runs over it in a fall.

backstepping the rope Allowing the rope to trail behind the leg or foot while lead climbing, creating the potential for inverting the climber in the event of a fall.

belay anchor Attachment point used to secure the belayer to the ground. See also *floor anchor*.

belay device Piece of equipment used by the belayer to increase the running friction of the rope and to keep the climber safe.

belay gloves Close-fitting leather gloves that give the belayer an added layer of protection from the rope.

belay loop Nylon loop of webbing attaching the waist belt and leg loops of the harness.

belay stance The belayer's body positioning. An athletic stance with one foot slightly in front of the other and knees bent, ready to absorb the force of the climber's fall.

belay test Competency test that each gym gives to climbers to ensure proper belay skills.

belayer Individual who manages the rope for the climber and keeps the rope from moving in the event of a fall.

belayer's neck Neck soreness from looking up too much at the climber while belaying.

"Belay's off" Belayer's acknowledgment that he is not belaying the climber any more.

"Belay on" Response from the belayer to the climber confirming the belayer is ready to belay.

bent-gate carabiners Carabiners with a curved gate to make clipping the rope easier.

bicycle move Often performed on steep terrain or roofs, one foot pushes against a hold while the other foot toe-hooks the same hold to stabilize the body.

bight Loop of rope.

board lasted Describes a climbing shoe constructed around a stiff board above the sole.

bouldering Climbing unroped on boulders or traversing low to the ground. Often associated with very difficult, although short bursts, of climbing.

bouldering pad Large pad used to cushion the impact of a boulderer's fall. Also called *crash pad*.

brake hand Hand used to brake the climber in the event of a fall. It is always in contact with the brake strand and is usually the belayer's dominant hand.

brake position Positioning the brake hand below the belay device with a firm grip to keep the rope from moving.

brake strand End of the rope that extends from the belay device and is held by the belayer's brake hand.

carabiner Aluminum (can be steel) clip with a spring-loaded gate, used to attach climbing equipment and ropes together.

chalk bag Hand-sized bag attached to the harness or a belt, filled with gymnastic chalk as a drying element for the hands.

chalk ball Mesh ball filled with chalk. Some gyms only allow chalk balls in order to minimize the amount of loose chalk dust indoors.

"Climb on" Confirmation from the belayer to the climber that the climber is ascending.

"Climbing" Spoken by the climber to let the belayer know that she is about to climb.

core The middle structure of a climbing rope comprised of tiny filaments, providing the elastic properties of the rope.

crash pad See *bouldering pad*.

crimping Grabbing an edge with the hands by placing the fingertips on the hold and buckling the knuckles under the pressure of weighting the hold.

crossing through Positioning the hands or feet across the body to minimize frontal positioning.

crux Hardest part of a climb or boulder problem.

deadpoint The point where a climber's center of gravity is motionless during a dynamic move, just after moving up and before coming back down.

difficulty competitions Events in which winning is based on how high or far the climbers ascend. These competitions are either top-roped or sport climbing.

dihedral The inside of a corner.

doubled-back The final stage of securing a harness buckle in which half of the buckle is covered with webbing.

double bowline Tie-in knot often used by lead and sport climbers because it is easy to untie after being weighted by a lead fall. Also called a *sport bowline*.

draw See *quickdraw*.

dressing Configuring a knot to minimize rope twists or to adjust segment lengths.

drop knee Rotating the knee toward the midline to help rotate the hips and twist the body.

dynamic movement Momentum-based movement often generated by the climber's center of gravity.

dyno Dynamic movement. Often used to describe extremely long moves in which the hands and feet lose contact with the wall.

edging Stepping on a hold using the edge of the foot.

external imagery Visualization based on viewing yourself as if someone were video-taping and you were watching the results on a video monitor.

"Falling" Spoken by a climber to let the belayer know he is falling.

feeding rope When the belayer gives out slack to the climber.

figure eight follow-through An easy to identify knot commonly used by the climber to tie in to the rope. Also called a *figure eight retrace*.

figure eight retrace See *figure eight follow-through*.

fingerboard See *hangboard*.

fingerlock Placing the fingertips into a crack and rotating the entire hand to lock the fingers in the crack.

flagging Placing the inside or outside edge of the foot against the wall for stability.

flash ascent Completing a route on the first try without falling or weighting the rope but with prior knowledge of the route.

flash pump An overaccumulation of lactic acid from not properly warming up.

floor anchor Ground attachment point in climbing gyms to keep the belayer affixed to the floor. See also *belay anchor*.

flow The ability to string multiple, uninterrupted moves together.

foot jam Sliding the foot into a crack as far as it will go and rotating the knee so it points straight up and the foot turns down, securing the hold. See also *toe jam*.

frontal positioning Climbing with the shoulders and hips square and with the center of gravity close to the wall. The inside edges of the feet are used and the knees are turned out.

gaston A type of "pushing" sidepull where the positive part of the hold is facing the climber.

gate The moving part of a carabiner that opens and shuts.

gear loops Plastic or nylon loops attached to a harness's waist belt, used for clipping carabiners and gear.

grade Describes a route or boulder problem's difficulty. In indoor climbing, interchangeable with *rating*.

GriGri Autocamming (autolocking) belay device that is popular among gym and sport climbers.

guide hand The belayer's free hand, or the one not used for braking.

gym climbing Indoor climbing on an artificial climbing wall.

half of a double fisherman Acceptable backup knot for the figure eight follow-through or double bowline.

hand and foot match Placing a foot on the same hold that a hand is already on.

hand jam Placing the entire hand into a crack and squeezing the hand to allow it to expand and stay placed.

hangboard Shoulder-width handhold with multiple hand grips used for developing hand and upper-body conditioning. Also called a *fingerboard*.

harness Padded webbing seat used to attach the climber or belayer to the rope or other safety anchors. Also used for attaching climbing gear.

heel hook Placing the heel of the foot on top or around a foothold to pull the hips in over the hold.

high step Placing the foot high up the wall, often requiring the stepping knee to be turned out to keep the hips close to the wall.

internal imagery Visualization from the perspective of seeing your environment as if you were on the route.

jib Small, moveable screw-in footholds often found in bouldering areas that give climbers more options for footholds.

lace-up shoes Climbing shoes with a traditional lacing system that extends down to the toe rand. These shoes offer the most adjustment of fit.

last Shaped footprint of a climbing shoe.

lead anchors Final anchors of a lead climb that the leader must clip the rope through to be lowered.

lead climbing Form of roped climbing in which the climber's rope trails down to the belayer below. The climber periodically attaches the rope to pieces of protective gear fixed to the rock or wall.

leg loops Leg straps that are a part of the harness and that fit on the upper thigh. Some are adjustable.

"Lower" Spoken by the climber to let the belayer know that she wants to be lowered.

matching Placing either both hands or both feet on the same hold.

muscular balance Having a proportionally appropriate amount of strength between climbing-specific and seldom-used muscles. Muscular imbalance can lead to injury.

muscular endurance The ability to generate strength multiple times.

muscular strength Amount of force generated by a muscle or group of muscles.

"Off belay" What the climber says after he is back on the ground and no longer in need of a belayer.

"On belay" Spoken by the climber to confirm that the belayer is ready to protect the climber.

onsight ascent Climbing a route from start to finish without falling or weighting the rope without any prior knowledge of the route, including watching others.

open hand Grabbing a hold using a relaxed hand grip, in which the fingers are fairly straight.

overhang A face that leans toward the climber, forcing the climber to put more weight on her upper body.

periodization Variations in the intensity, duration, mode, and frequency of training.

pinching Using the thumb to squeeze the entire hand while grabbing a hold.

pocket A hold that has an indentation in which to fit the fingers or the toes.

power The amount of work performed divided by the amount of time it takes to perform the work.

problem A bouldering route.

quickdraw Two carabiners attached to one another by a piece of nylon webbing, used to clip in to on sport climbs. Also called a *draw*.

rand Thin rubber extending above the sole of the climbing shoe. The toe rand can be replaced.

rating Numerical system describing a route or boulder problem's difficulty. Also called *grade* in indoor climbing; see also *Yosemite Decimal System* and *V-scale*.

redpoint ascent Completing a route without falling or weighting the rope, having already made a first attempt.

resole The process of replacing the worn-down sole of a climbing shoe with a new sole.

rise Distance between the harness's waist belt and leg loops.

route setter Person who positions holds on a climbing wall to design a route or a boulder problem.

sequencing Determining where to go, which hand- and footholds to use, and proper body positioning on a climb.

setting Tightening a knot by hand immediately after tying it in order to minimize knot slippage at a later time.

sharp end The lead climber's end of the rope.

sheath Loosely woven protective casing surrounding a climbing rope's core.

sidepull A sideways-positioned handhold that requires the climber to lean away from the hold to create enough opposition for stability.

slab Less-than-vertical climbing terrain.

"Slack" This command is used when the climber needs more rope from the belayer.

slip-lasted Describes a climbing shoe constructed with a sensitive last slipped in.

slippers Laceless climbing shoes that offer the most sensitivity. They must be sized extremely tight to minimize the foot sliding around inside.

sloper A hold that slopes down and away from the wall and that is often difficult to hold onto.

smearing Positioning the sole of the foot against the wall by lowering the heel to increase the surface area and pressure between the sole and wall.

speed-climbing competitions Competitions in which the winner is the climber who ascends the fastest. These are top-rope events.

sport bowline See *double bowline*.

sport climbing Form of lead climbing in which the climber attaches the rope to fixed, permanent bolts and anchors on the rock or wall. All gym lead climbing is sport climbing.

static movement In-control movement sustained by the climber's muscles. A good indication of static movement is whether or not the climber can stop at any point during the move.

stemming Pushing the hands or feet in opposition, often in a corner.

straight-gate carabiners Carabiners with a traditionally straight gate. A multiuse carabiner.

tail Amount of rope that extends from a knot to the end of the rope.

"Take" The climber's command telling the belayer to take the climber's weight on the rope.

toe hook Using the top part of the foot or toes to hook around a foothold. Often used on steep, overhanging terrain.

toe jam Inserting the toes into a crack and turning the foot down to lock the toes in place, securing the hold. See also *foot jam*.

top-roping A roped climbing system in which the climbing rope travels up to an above anchor and then back down to the belayer.

tracking Climbing indoors using only the hand- and footholds that are designated as a part of the route being attempted.

traversing Horizontal climbing often done close to the ground and without a rope.

tubular belay device A generally light-weight, manually locking belay device that a majority of climbers use for belaying.

twistlocking Twisting the hips and body and ultimately locking the arm to allow the reaching arm to extend.

UIAA Union Internationale des Associations d'Alpinisme. International organization governing the safety standards of climbing gear.

undercling Handhold that is grabbed on the bottom, with the reaching hand's palm facing the climber.

"Up rope" Spoken by the climber to the belayer, announcing that slack needs to be taken up.

Velcro shoes Climbing shoes with Velcro closures. Easy to put on and take off, and they allow fit adjustments.

visualization Mental imagery of climbing performance.

V-scale Bouldering rating scale ranging from V0 to V15.

waist belt Uppermost part of the harness that snugly fits around the smallest part of the waist.

waiver of liability Legal agreement that must be signed by the participant (or participant's parent or legal guardian if a minor) acknowledging the risks of climbing indoors.

webbing Usually nylon, woven flat like a strap or belt. See also *quickdraw*.

weight shifting Controlling the center of gravity to properly keep weight over the legs and feet.

wire-gate carabiners Carabiners with gates made of looped wire, for lighter weight and less movement.

Yosemite Decimal System (YDS) Rating system for climbing routes. All indoor, roped climbing routes have a prefix of 5 and the number after the decimal designates the difficulty from 1 to 15. Climbs higher than 5.10 may be further categorized with a through d.

Z-clip Results when quickdraws are clipped in the incorrect order, forcing the rope into a Z-shaped line and creating tremendous rope drag.

INDEX

ABOUT THE AUTHOR

Matt Burbach has been a climbing instructor since 1995. He is currently the editor of *Urban Climber Magazine,* a publication dedicated to bouldering, sport climbing, gym, and competition climbing. He established, developed, and directed the indoor climbing school at Earth Treks Climbing Center in Maryland, the largest climbing gym on the east coast. Matt has worked in the climbing industry as an instructor, competitor, tech rep, and lead organizer of the Petzl Roc Comp and Smackdown competitions. He graduated from the University of Maryland College of Health and Human Performance and continues to coach climbers on an individual basis. Matt currently lives in the Washington, D.C. area with his wife, Elizabeth.

(Photo by Sue Borchardt)

THE MOUNTAINEERS, founded in 1906, is a nonprofit outdoor activity and conservation club, whose mission is "to explore, study, preserve, and enjoy the natural beauty of the outdoors . . . ." The club sponsors many classes and year-round outdoor activities in the Pacific Northwest, and supports environmental causes through educational activities, sponsoring legislation and presenting educational programs. The Mountaineers Books supports the club's mission by publishing travel and natural history guides, instructional texts, and works on conservation and history.

Send or call for our catalog of more than 500 outdoor titles:

The Mountaineers Books
1001 SW Klickitat Way, Suite 201
Seattle, WA 98134
800-553-4453
mbooks@mountaineersbooks.org
www.mountaineersbooks.org

The Mountaineers Books is proud to be a corporate sponsor of The Leave No Trace Center for Outdoor Ethics, whose mission is to promote and inspire responsible outdoor recreation through education, research, and partnerships. The Leave No Trace program is focused specifically on human-powered (nonmotorized) recreation.
  Leave No Trace strives to educate visitors about the nature of their recreational impacts, as well as to offer techniques to prevent and minimize such impacts. Leave No Trace is best understood as an educational and ethical program, not as a set of rules and regulations.
  For more information, visit *www.LNT.org,* or call 800-332-4100.

OTHER TITLES IN THE MOUNTAINEERS OUTDOOR EXPERT SERIES

Climbing: From Gym to Crag, *S. Peter Lewis & Dan Cauthorn*
Climbing: Training for Peak Performance, *Clyde Soles*
Rock Climbing: Mastering Basic Skills, *Craig Luebben*
Alpine Climbing: Techniques to Take You Higher, *Mark Houston & Kathy Cosley*
Ice & Mixed Climbing: Modern Technique, *Will Gadd*
Big Wall Climbing: Elite Technique, *Jared Ogden*
Climbing: Expedition Planning, *Clyde Soles & Phil Powers*

OTHER TITLES YOU MIGHT ENJOY FROM THE MOUNTAINEERS BOOKS

Mountaineering: The Freedom of the Hills, *The Mountaineers*
The climber's bible—complete, authoritative instruction in an easy-to-use format.

The Outdoor Knots Book, *Clyde Soles.*
A guide to the ropes and knots used in the outdoors by hikers, campers, paddlers, and climbers. One of the best resources for climbing knots available.

Fifty Favorite Climbs: The Ultimate North American Tick List, *Mark Kroese*
Fifty elite climbers share their favorite routes—a celebration of contemporary climbing history and the climbers who have shaped it.

Available at fine bookstores and outdoor stores, by phone at 800-553-4453 or on the Web at *www.mountaineersbooks.org*

THE MOUNTAINEERS BOOKS